CONVICTED
OR CONDEMNED?

CONVICTED OR CONDEMNED?

Dez Brown
with Martin Saunders

Authentic

Copyright © 2005 Dez Brown and Martin Saunders

26 25 24 23   8 7 6 5

First published 2005 by Authentic Media
PO Box 6326, Bletchley, Milton Keynes, Bucks,
MK1 9GG, UK, and
129 Mobilization Drive, Waynesboro, GA 30830-4575, USA

Reprinted 2016, 2017, 2022, 2023

The right of Dez Brown and Martin Saunders to be identified
as the authors of this work has been asserted by them in accor-
dance with the Copyright, Designs and Patents Act 1988.

British Library Cataloguing in Publication Data

A catalogue record for this book is available from the British
Library

978-1-86024-484-1

All Scripture quotations are from the
HOLY BIBLE, NEW INTERNATIONAL VERSION.
Copyright © 1973, 1978, 1984 by International Bible Society.
Used by permission of Hodder & Stoughton, a member of
Hodder Headline Ltd. All rights reserved.

Cover design and photography by Andy Colthart
www.jharts.co.uk
Print Management by Adare Carwin
Printed and bound by CPI Group (UK) Ltd, Croydon, CR0 4YY

ONE

I killed a man

This is the story, of how I, Desmond Brown, fell so far that before I was 18 years old, I was running away from the screams of a dying man, with a bloody knife clenched in my hand. It is the story of how, in just a few short years, I managed to develop an attitude and mindset that was truly dark, truly criminal, truly evil.

And yet it is the story of how in the midst of that darkness, light appeared. It is the story of how, somehow, I managed to turn the great hulking wreck that was my life, around. It is the story, of a life completely restored.

This is my story.

*   *   *

I was born in 1973, and spent the early years of my life in Chadwell Heath, Essex. My mum and dad were married, and, along with my older brother, we all lived in a two-bedroom house. My dad, who came originally from Kingston, Jamaica, worked for Ford, and my mum, who came from the slightly less exotic Braintree area of Essex, was a nurse, working with patients who had mental health issues. In the 1970s it was quite unusual, socially speaking, to have a black man married to a white woman, and in Chadwell Heath. I wasn't aware of it as I was growing up, but my colour made me quite distinct because there weren't many black, and especially mixed-race, children around. For that reason, if ever we got into fights, my mum would often encourage us to go out there and 'look after ourselves', because she didn't want us to become the victims of racism or bullying.

In that spirit of self-defence, my brother Elton and I would go to Judo lessons each week. It was a long way away but we enjoyed it so much, and were quite good at it, that we didn't mind having to walk so far. Both my brother and I won a few trophies. However, because we were both quite big and strong for our age, when we went into a category to fight people of our own age we'd beat black belts purely because of our strength. It certainly wasn't to do with technique – we were both just big, strong boys.

I enjoyed an eventful childhood and had good friends around me. But for some reason, I seemed to be magnetically attracted to crime and violence. For instance – perhaps the very earliest example – I remember being involved in an armed robbery when I was very young, at the local post office. I was just a small child – no, I wasn't the one doing the hold up – and a guy came in with a mask and a shotgun. I was just in there buying sweets but he told me and everyone else to keep down and keep still. He took all the money from the till and got away. Even though I was young and brave, I never once thought about trying to save the day. I just sat there on the floor, cowering, and thinking 'Wow! This is amazing!' I found the experience exciting, like this guy was some kind of outlaw. Afterwards I ran home, excited by the big story I had to tell my mum. 'Mum, Mum!' I shouted as I came through the door. 'I've just been involved in a robbery!'

I became friends with a boy who lived near that post office and, again, violence seemed to follow me. Once I was playing with him in his back garden and started messing around with a hammer. Now I realise that this is not a sensible thing to do. Back then, I thought it might be fun to hit things with it. So I ended up hitting myself on the thumb, and passed out from the pain.

My infant school was fun. I was well-liked within the school. Even the headmistress liked me and I was quite a good boy. I didn't get into any trouble there. My only memories of the place are the most distinctive ones: when I was there the school was undergoing improvements so we were taught in huts; and we used to be given a carton of free milk every day! The other thing about that place was that the boys and girls shared communal toilets, a memory which, for some reason, remains with me to this day.

When I was still quite young I got bitten by a neighbour's dog. This dog had a nappy on, because it had the runs – it had one of those owners who doted far too much on their animal. They knew I was scared of the dog, but they let him out into their garden when I was there, to go to the toilet. So they took the nappy off, and the dog came running out towards me. It could tell that I was scared of it – it was staring at me and I was staring back. I called its name – I was probably being a bit unwise there – and it came running at me full-pelt. I ran to try to get to the stile that would take me out of the garden, but before I could get there the dog caught me, and bit me. So one end of the dog was clamped on to me, and the other end was doing what comes naturally when you've got the runs. I would have laughed if it hadn't been my leg. My mum and dad could hear me screaming, so my mum came out of our house, a couple of doors down, to rescue me. I had to go to hospital for eight stitches.

After that, I went on to a linked primary and secondary school called Warren Comprehensive. It was a bit of a walk from home, although the school field backed on to the end of my road. You got told off by the neighbours or the school if you bunked over the fence, so I didn't do it . . . not, at least, until I was a bit older. The only time we'd ever risk it was when there was a school fête on – because then we could get there early and get all the good toys.

Long before my criminal mindset came along, I developed a love of fighting which, perhaps, was born out of learning self-defence. As a young secondary-schooler, I never used to go looking for fights, but then, on the other hand, I would never back down from one if challenged. I'd had fights from a fairly young age. The first significant one was with a boy in my brother's year. They called him 'Zammo', after a character in *Grange Hill*, which was a TV programme big at the time. He was very troublesome at school, just like Zammo. I came running off a merry-go-round and he took me out. He was one of the key people in the school – more because of his mouth and his designer clothes than anything else. I got up and asked, 'What did you do that for?'

And he punched me in the face. So we got into this fight and, to cut a long story short, I beat him up. I got him in a head-lock and I just kept kneeing him in the face. My trousers got completely covered in blood. Everyone was around us, watching. This was a significant thing: he was two years older than me, and everyone saw this young kid batter him, quite badly. He went off crying, and I went off home, my adrenaline pumping, and told my mum the story. She gave me extra pocket money, because she'd always told me to look after myself. First of all she asked, 'Did you start the fight?' and I said, 'No'. Once she'd ascertained that, she said, 'Well done for looking after yourself.' From that point on, I was known in the school as someone who could put up a fight. Suddenly I wasn't just Big Elton's brother – suddenly I was Dez. My brother was known in the school – although not particularly in the area outside it – not because he was a fighter, but because he was quite big. People don't mess with you when you're 13 or 14 and big.

I had a few more fights in school. A more violent streak began to emerge in me. I started to form the capacity to be nasty. I had this friend – of course, my actions towards him proved that I didn't really know what that word meant – but I called him a friend. His dad owned a sweet shop, and when I found that out, I discussed the idea of taking money from the shop so that we could go up to the West End and buy things with it. He lived in this sweet shop, and I'd say to him, 'Give me £20.' Now in those days, the mid 1980s, £20 was a lot of money.

Or he'd take a whole box of football stickers and an album, and we'd go to this place we called 'the dump' and open up all the little packets and fill up the album. That led to a taste for getting money and free stuff, and so what I used to do was bully him to get more money. I think it was at that point that an 'evil' streak began to develop in me. I got a taste for manipulation and control. I'd arrange to stand in the alley by the shop, and he'd chuck a bag of pound coins over the fence. He'd nicked them from his dad – sometimes because he wanted to, but more often because I was putting pressure on him. Then it got bigger to the point that I'd say, 'Right, go and get £50, and we'll go and buy a stereo.' Then I'd pretend to my mum and dad that I'd found this stereo in the park – just left there. Then it went further: 'Get £100'; 'Get £150'. I'd go home and tell my parents, 'I've found this money!' I even set it all up really believably – I went out and bought a wallet, filled it with the money and then told my parents I'd found the wallet in the street. I even put dust and leaves in the wallet to add realism.

I don't know why or how I learned to lie – I just picked up that if I wanted something, lying was often a good tool for getting it. I hadn't been influenced by a single incident or person to cause me to act this way – in fact my dad was the closest you could get to a vicar without being one. He had clear morals: he never swore; never lied; never did anyone wrong. My parents loved me – they disciplined me as well – and they gave me the right amount of freedom. So I could never look back and say that what came later was because of this or that in my upbringing. I had a very good, stable upbringing. It was just a sinister, selfish, evil streak that grew within me when I saw that I could get what I wanted if I broke a few rules.

So I took the money – £150 – from my 'friend', went into the local supermarket to buy a cheap wallet, and worked myself up to tell a convincing lie. Then I went home and told my parents, 'I've found a wallet – I've found a wallet!' I knew what I wanted to buy, too – there was this BMX bike that cost £110. I even made a big gesture to my parents – I let them keep the other £40! So I went out and bought my BMX with the dirty money. But crime doesn't always pay – at least my one didn't. The bike got stolen a few weeks later.

I don't think my friend's dad ever knew the full extent of what had been taken. All I know is that a little while after that, he came marching up the high street, looking for me. He saw me – he was this very short Asian man (significantly short) – and he shouted at me, and then delivered a huge slap to my face. It was deserved, obviously, and I think even I knew it. Then he simply told me to keep away from his son, and walked calmly away. And that was it.

When I was 12, I got stabbed by a guy armed with a bottle. Me, the sweet shop guy and another friend were casually passing the time like any other innocent kids – lobbing water balloons at buses and, occasionally, people. One of our victims was a young guy, about 13 or 14, who didn't take kindly to being drenched. He ran over to us and set upon my friend. I was bigger than my friend, so I said, 'Don't trouble my friend, trouble me.' That had seemed like a cool thing to say at the time. We got into this fight – this, really vicious fight – where we were biting one another. It was the most venomous fight I'd ever had – if we'd had a shot at poking the other's eye out, we would have taken it. This fight went on for ten or fifteen minutes, and we ended up rolling around in the rocks and the dirt. In the end, I got the upper hand, and he ran off. I got up thinking, '*Yeah, I've won this fight.*' But then my friend shrieked at me, 'Dez – look at your side!' I looked down, and there was blood all over my T-shirt. I pulled up the shirt and I had this massive gaping wound on my side. I staggered home in shock, but my mum and dad weren't there. I had to go to my neighbour's house instead, and they called the ambulance for me. Just before it arrived, my mum and dad appeared and came with me to hospital where I got another twelve stitches and a scar to go with the one that Diarrhoea Dog had given me. After that, I was even more interested in fighting, and being able to defend myself.

We used to fire catapults at buses. We used to hang around in 'the dump': a building site that had been left derelict for a while, and we used it as our base. We'd hide behind the mounds on the site, and build little camps for ourselves. We had catapults called 'black widows' – and when the buses came past we'd fire them and they wouldn't know where the shot had come from. We smashed so many windows, stopped so many buses and made so many people late! But we didn't care. That was fun to us.

When I was 15, I befriended this bloke who worked in the local video shop. We said to him, 'Give us some of your old videos, and we'll rent them at school.' He began to give us some of the old '18s' that no one rented anymore. We'd go to school with ten or twelve videos in our bags, and we'd either sell or rent them. That was a good racket for a while, but the films weren't that good and so we grew greedy. We started asking for more videos – we wanted the up-to-date ones, so that we could rent them out at a premium. Obviously, he didn't want to give us these – he didn't want to get into trouble with his boss – and he told us 'No'. So we beat him up, really badly, breaking a couple of his ribs. Naturally, we didn't go back to the shop, but the man who owned it came looking for us in the park. He came running after us, but we managed to escape. The guy himself didn't want to press charges – he was scared of the repercussions – and so, again, it never went any further.

We'd go up to Romford, the nearest big town, and steal from shops. Not because I needed to but because I wanted to – there were a few things I wanted that I didn't have, but I always had plenty of what I needed. So we'd go into a shop and take a jacket, or some headphones, and now and then we might get chased. I got caught once, and my parents had to come up to collect me from the shop.

Generally, though, my parents were oblivious to all of this. It just never came to the surface – no one grassed on me, I rarely got caught; in school I did enough work to avoid the teachers' special attention (it wasn't good, but it was average) and was never kicked out or suspended. I was rarely late home – I usually told my parents where I'd be (even if I was lying slightly). But it was a completely different world that I lived in, and my parents were never made to visit. My parents were good parents, but I masked my badness very well.

A lot of my friends were more problematic in school than me, and therefore their parents knew what they got up to. I was wiser than that – more calculating. I knew how to act around people: I knew how to say 'please', 'thank you', 'I'm sorry' and generally how to be a nice boy. Around teachers or relatives I was never out of hand. Even in the incidents where I got caught, such as the shoplifting or when I smashed someone's window, I just denied everything. I learned that the words, 'It wasn't us' could be very valuable, and because I knew how to be good and sweet to the right people, they believed me.

It was a massive window – a great double-glazed thing. I was pretending to throw a discus – with a big rock as a substitute – but I messed up my technique and ended up throwing it directly in the one direction that I was trying not to. It shattered this massive window, several feet high and wide. We tried to calmly walk away but the security guards had seen us do it, so they escorted us back and waited with us for the police. We had to spend an evening in the cells, and our parents were called. We just said, 'We didn't do it – it wasn't us.' Now we didn't *intend* to do it, but we did it alright. There's a big difference between the two. But again, because they had no evidence, we got away with it.

At 14, I was supremely confident in myself, especially around those that I knew, and around my own area. I had no real enemies; I got on with people, was well-liked and had a lot of friends. I was aware of my sinister streak, bubbling away under the surface, yet, while I had it under control, I was also feeding it. And by that time, I'd begun to realise my colour – that I was black. At that age, I started to go further afield on an evening out – ice-skating in Romford. And that was where we'd meet the black gangs, from Stratford and Forrest Gate. In my school there weren't many black people, so during the day I'd have a mixture of friends, but in the evening, my friendships with young black people began to define who I was. My identity had already begun to take root in my music – rap and ragga. I was beginning to find what I thought was 'my culture'. And my influences, not that I needed anything to further steer me in the wrong direction, were quite negative role models. These were people who were smoking weed, and selling various drugs.

So by the age of 15, my criminal mindset had already taken shape. I'd learned to fight and over-power others, but much more significantly, I'd learned how to manipulate. I had become calculat-ing, and could use lies and pressure to get people to do what I wanted. Things went well for me, in a perverse sort of way, and I realised that these atti-tudes and techniques would pay me well. Perhaps there would be a price to pay in the future, but if I continued to be clever, and stayed in control, I thought I was pretty well invincible.

TWO

From about the age of 15 I started to develop another circle of black friends who weren't from my area. It didn't mean that I couldn't hang around with my school friends, but they just wanted to hang around on street corners and get drunk, messing around, and this didn't really appeal to me. With my new friends I could get involved in going ice-skating until midnight and raving (dance music gatherings), which were a lot more fun. Now when I say 'raving', I'm talking more about house parties than the big illegal club raves, because, even though I was clear on my culture and identity, going to that sort of rave could be quite intimidating. That kind of environment was tense, with lots of drug-taking going on, and everyone there wanting to be the thug. I did go sometimes, and the kind of vibe that you'd get would be everyone stirring up each other, like hundreds of prowling lions circling and baiting each other. You'd go into the hallway and there'd be people kind of lined up all along the wall. My friends and I would appear, and people would be asking, 'Who is this?' My friends and I would dress flamboyantly, which attracted attention, and then there was the fact that I was light-skinned. Back then, there was a real distinction between someone being mixed race and someone being black, because, at that point, the mixed race boys were seen as the 'sweet boys'. And the colours in which we dressed really did make us stand out. We mostly chose those colours out of personal taste, but there was also an element of wanting people to notice us. We certainly achieved that objective.

The music predominantly played at these raves was ragga, which was the style of music that I was most interested in and keen on. Although we'd go to raves where they'd play soul or acid, the kind of music popular at that time, it wasn't really my thing. I mean, I could dance to it a bit, but when it came down to it, the music didn't connect with me – I was a ragga man. The artists I was into then were Ninjaman, General Levy and Papa San. The music was dark, with explicit and violent content, and I'd be foolish to think that this didn't have an influence on my mindset. It was the biggest purely Caribbean influence on me, and was fuelled by my half-sister's (one of two from my dad's first marriage) frequent trips to Jamaica. We would get hold of 'sound tapes' direct from Jamaica, which were raw and unedited.

Sound tapes were actually recorded live at an open-air rave, so you'd get all the swearing and all the gun shots left in. We saw this as 'the good stuff'. They were the hard-core tapes and not many people in my circle of friends could get them.

I was also into rap and hip-hop. Rap wasn't something I could do, but my brother, who was more into that sort of music, could. Elton got hold of all my music, so I appreciated the stuff he was into, too. At times he'd let me borrow his decks and play our tunes.

The music helped me to become increasingly aware of, and place greater importance on, my colour. And even though I was of mixed race, I began to see myself as black, and saw this as key to my identity. I hung around in a black group more and more, while my view of white people became, admittedly, quite skewed. I didn't, for instance, ever perceive white girls to be racist, perhaps because my mum was white. And one of my closest friends, Danny, was a white guy. But at the same time, I became more suspicious of white males.

I became more aware of actual racial tension when I went to Romford ice rink, where there was kind of a National Front (NF) contingent. Romford, Barking and Dagenham, were predominantly white areas, and certain areas, particularly of Dagenham, were very 'white' and known for being 'niffy' (racist). On a few occasions, we would get chased by groups of white men. They were just doing it for a laugh, but from our point of view we were running for our lives. We were 14, 15 or 16 years old, and they were all 18-plus. They'd shout, 'Niggers! – Get 'em!'

There was a pub in Romford called the Birdcage, which was known for being niffy. We'd just be walking past on our way back from ice-skating, and they'd all pile out and chase us. It happened more than once, and so this couldn't help but shape my view of white people.

But, of course, it works both ways. There was a time when lots of people got robbed – usually the black kids robbing the white kids. But it would also happen black against black – sometimes I got approached, for instance. At other times, we would walk past a group of men and just for a laugh we'd throw milk bottles at them, and get chased. I don't think things were all that bad, and I never had the time or maturity to reason in my head that my opinions were based on prejudice – it was just what happened. I didn't walk around feeling paranoid because of my colour – but I was aware. I was never ignorant enough to say 'all white people are racist'. I was brought up by and around white people. It was more that I viewed certain areas of London as a bit 'niffy'. It was the areas, not the people, that I identified as racist.

At 16, I started at Waltham Forest College – the college my brother attended. I'd never really been to Walthamstow, and I didn't have any friends going there. I was doing a first diploma in construction, because I wanted to be a quantity surveyor. A close friend of the family who was in that line of business had given me summer work experience. I'd worked with them as a quantity surveyor – not doing all the stuff that they did, but just helping out. They'd said to me, 'There'll always be a job here for you if you pass your exams,' so I decided to go into it.

I made friends quite quickly. I was a lot more independent, and the culture was much more complicated than at school. There were lots of more mature girls on the scene and, at the same time, plenty of enemies, who seemed to take exception to me because I was popular with the girls and dressed loudly. I became a well-known figure in the college quite quickly, but not necessarily for the right reasons. Part of it was because of my looks and the way I dressed, and part of it was down to the way in which I behaved.

I wasn't stupid though. I was streetwise and retained an attitude around my peers, but at the same time I knew when to get my head down and work. I was calculating in the way I conducted myself. I didn't just walk around like I was the big man all the time, because sometimes that would bring negative attention, and I'd get myself whacked by someone bigger and stronger. But, nevertheless, I knew how to hold my own.

I'd been attracted to girls from the age of 12 or 13. Although at times in my early teens I got involved in relationships, my attitude to girls wasn't great. I had a one-track mind and I was always looking out for what I could get, how dating them benefited me, and how good they looked on my arm. I didn't really engage my feelings, and so relationships then were more about status than anything else. I can even remember having a competition with Elton to see who could go out with the most girls at one time (he won, he had eleven and I had nine). So I'd never really had a serious relationship by the time I arrived at college.

Part of the way into my first year at college, I was in the midst of another of those non-serious, status relationships. However, at the same time, there was one girl in the college who made me feel different. Her name was Sheila, and she was studying a different course to me. When I'd see her around, she and I used to just stare at one another from across the college. We never spoke – it was like a strange kind of courting ritual. It happened a lot, this staring game. The first time that we maintained significant eye contact, I went out of my way to let her know that I was looking at her, and just kept staring. She decided that she wasn't going to be the one to look away first, and so as we walked along, a hundred metres apart on different sides of the college grounds, we were locked in this visual embrace . . . until she nearly walked into a parked car, which kind of killed the moment.

Like me, Sheila was very distinctive in the way that she dressed. This was mainly because she got her clothes handmade – although she wouldn't tell anyone where. Her look – both in terms of her clothes and her face – was what really attracted me to her, but she also had a confidence and attitude which I found appealing. She didn't hang around with the wrong crowd. She presented herself – in street terms of the time – as a 'rude girl', but she wasn't actually one, and she didn't hang out with the rude girls. Like me, she was there to study, she was there to do her work. She wasn't loud and in-your-face or the mouthy one. She was very quiet, very very beautiful, and she stuck out. She was special, and I knew I couldn't just have her if I wanted to. Before long I had become smitten, and even told a few of my friends.

I didn't know it until that point, but her brothers were very well known in the area, more for the wrong reasons. My friends asked me if I was sure about this, knowing who her brothers were. After all, this wasn't the kind of girl you just messed around with – there were consequences, a few strings attached. That was neither here nor there for me, though. I liked her, and I didn't know them, so I didn't care. I hadn't done anything wrong and my intentions weren't to do so. Anyway, my attitude towards relationships had matured and I wouldn't have just taken advantage of someone. For once, I really wanted to go out with her, and not just have a fling.

I realised from her body language, and the grapevine, that the attraction was mutual – but there was a catch. When I spoke to her, she told me that unless I let go of my other girlfriend, then it couldn't happen between us. Incredibly, that was the first time that anyone had ever actually said that to me, and it came as a bit of a shock. So I had to make a decision: did I dump this girl and get together with Sheila, or did I try to run with two? Running with two would have been difficult – they were both in the same college! I decided to respect

Sheila for what she said, and I finished the other relationship.

So Sheila and I became an item. Very quickly, though, I realised that this was not going to be the easiest relationship in the world. I called her house one night when she wasn't there. Instead, her older brother answered.

'Who's this?' he growled.

'It's Dez.'

'Why you calling?' he spluttered. 'Who are you? Dez who?' It was 'Twenty Questions'.

Despite some of my failings, I wasn't arrogant or unwise. I knew how to play the game. I was polite, because I knew that I had to make an impression, and I didn't want to make an enemy of my girl-friend's brother. Again, it was calculated.

He still wasn't happy but then, being quite a bit older, he didn't accept any of Sheila's boyfriends. And because Sheila had grown up without a dad, he'd played a father-figure role. What he said, she would have done. So she had to start by saying that we were friends, and then slowly let him know that I was a boyfriend. But she didn't feel able to take me home if he was there at the same time.

Her other brother was only a little older than her and a lot more accepting of the idea of Sheila and me – but even he was stand-offish. Fortunately, he was more influenced by his girlfriend, who was a bit more supportive of Sheila being in a relationship. She helped to keep his nose out of it.

You might have thought that with a nice girl on my arm – and one that I actually cared about at that – I may have calmed down and chilled out at that point, but the opposite was the case. It was then that I started selling drugs in the college, and I also started getting involved in street robbery.

I'd started smoking drugs – cannabis or 'hash' – when I was about 14. At the age of 15, I had started taking LSD trips. Within another year, I was onto 'speed', too; it was a natural progression. Many people who do drugs regularly also begin to sell them to finance their habit, and so it was with me. I started selling hash in the college, and before long I got hold of cheaper hash because it was mixed with other stuff. So, although the quality of the stuff I was selling was pretty rubbish, I'd just sell it anyway because it got me money – and as I said before, I'd already developed a love for having plenty of that.

That was just part of my income though. I also worked on a market stall, where I used to take the money – not all the money, but a lot of the time it was a stupid percentage. I used to work at

Dagenham market, at a women's clothes stall. Quite often I'd be the only person working and I'd pocket the bulk of the takings. Sometimes I'd come back with £120 – and we'd only taken £200! After a while, though, it caught up with me and I got my just desserts; the owner had to let me go because she wasn't making enough money.

I didn't actually sell drugs for long – perhaps for two or three months. I got my supply through a friend of my brother. It was a good deal. I'd get it cheap, and it was easy, not like getting it from some hard-nosed dealer who might come round and break my legs if I didn't pay him. It wasn't loads, an ounce or two at a time, not kilos, and it was really just something I did because I wasn't getting much money from anywhere else.

Looking back, there was really no reason why I had to get involved in street robberies. I didn't need to – it was more of an image thing. This was where my sinister streak shone through. What began to happen was that I started to use my knife; it was a penknife that I'd bought from a fishing shop. Even for silly things, I'd threaten to stab someone. On one occasion, a lot later on, I actually stabbed someone because they wouldn't give me their ring. Even my friends began to realise that I was going a bit too far.

'What's he done to you?' they shouted at me. 'He's not going to give it to you – leave it now.'

I was threatening to take someone's life because of a ring. Right then I began to realise that I had a choice to make about how far I actually wanted to go with this. I think I'd always been in control; I had always been calculating. But now, with the power that holding a weapon brought, the situation became out of control and, to me, that was dangerous. I've always believed that if you keep your temper and remain calm, you can deal with any situation. Once you lose your temper, you lose control. That's when problems can arise that you didn't foresee or can't control. You don't want to lose control, and yet, when you do lose it, you realise that in fact you'd lost it a long time ago without really knowing.

Whereas before I'd been quite reserved in using my knife, I'd now become a bit more knife-happy. I didn't really respect or value somebody else's life. To me, the only life that was of any value was my own.

I didn't feel that I was out of control when I used hash. Obviously it made me quite drowsy and kind of chilled, but it didn't make me lose control. Trips could, but I'd never take more than one. I had friends that would take five or six, but not me – I couldn't be that out of control. I wasn't scared of death – I didn't really think death was part of the equation anyway – I just wasn't sure what would happen and I couldn't handle not knowing. To some, it was all about image – the more you took the harder you were – but that wasn't as important to me as being in control.

Although I messed around with them, drink and drugs weren't as big a part of my life as they were in some of my friends'. I didn't even smoke cigarettes because I didn't like the taste. I never really took cocaine – maybe because it was seen as the rich man's drug. But while they say you can't get addicted to cannabis, and physically maybe that's true, psychologically I was addicted. When I got up, I'd always have a spliff. I'd always have stuff with me. I'd always be buying it. In fact, at that time I felt like I couldn't live without it, but at the back of my mind there was always the knowledge that, in truth, I probably could.

Because of my calculating nature, I knew I could never allow myself to get too dependent on the stuff. I used it, but I didn't let it use me. But then, of course, spurred on by my drug habits, I did start to lose control.

THREE

Sheila and I weren't talking. I'd just come back from my sister's place in Brixton, and when I got in I got this call from Sheila. This was the first contact we'd had for a couple of weeks because we'd fallen out. She just said, 'Dez, you've got to come now, you've got to come now – your brother's face has been cut!'

She didn't know exactly what had happened, but she was crying on the other end of the phone and saying, 'He might have lost his eye'. All she'd seen was him covering his face, and blood gushing out everywhere. That was it. I said, 'Right, I'm coming,' and made my way out with my friend, Lee. We got ourselves tooled up (with weapons) – I usually was anyway by this stage – and headed for where they were.

I used to arm myself with a knife . . . and a fork! The knife was perhaps an obvious choice, but the fork was a home-made extra which I would bend around my fist so that the spikes were turned out towards any aggressor, and could be used for puncturing skin. It was like a primitive knuckleduster, but more vicious.

We travelled there – from Chadwell Heath to Forrest Gate – and got as far as Ilford, where we met Sheila. Because of the severity of the situation, we put our fall-out to one side and started talking again. She filled me in on the information, knowing that, obviously, the people who had cut my brother's face wouldn't still be there. It had happened at Wanstead Flats Fair. So I pieced together some information, asked around about Elton, then went home and told my mum and my dad. They spoke to him in the hospital and took over. The next morning I woke up and Elton was back home – with stitches in his face but, thankfully, with both eyes still intact. He was very quiet – psychologically scarred by it all – and it was at that point that we started talking about revenge.

'Right,' I said, 'we're going to get the bloke who did this.'

My family and friends were united – they all wanted to get this person.

My brother could fight, but he wasn't really a fighter. He'd never really needed to – mainly because he was so big. The fact that my older brother, who was bigger than me and who I looked up to, had had that done to his face made me feel that I was responsible for dealing with this. Of the two of us, I was more of the rude boy, living the street life – he was never into ragga music or the drugs. This wasn't the sort of thing that should have happened to him.

So we drove around for a few nights, trying to get the word from the street about who and where the guy who'd done this was. Because Elton had recently finished with a girl called Simone, we thought that it could have been linked to her. We even got a tip-off that said it was her cousin. We came very close to getting that guy. We got as far as finding out where he lived and planned to get him when he came out of his house. I wasn't there at the time, but my friends actually got hold of him and were about to 'do' him when he told them that it wasn't him, and gave them the name of the guy who had really done it. A short while after that we started talking to family members about taking a hit out on this guy. There was someone in our family who wasn't a hit man as such, but who lived life in the fast lane, and had done a few things like that before.

So we actually sat there around the family table.

Someone said, 'Well, how far do we go?'

'Do we want to kill him?' asked another. 'Do we want to do his legs?'

At that time, this was a case of my world colliding with reality. My parents were sitting there discussing this – which was very weird. What had happened was that they'd gradually become exposed, through snippets, to our world and to youth culture. And the way that they'd been exposed to it was through the way that we dressed, by the fact that we smoked drugs. I mean, they must have known; we used to smoke drugs in the house, upstairs, with the door shut and the window open. (Of course, I now know that if someone was sitting downstairs when you were doing that, they'd smell it through the door. And I'm not talking about one spliff here; I'm talking about ten people on a session, and everyone's smoking spliffs. I mean, when you were in there it was like a thick smog, and you could barely see who was on the other side of the room. You wouldn't have needed your own spliff, you could have just brought along a tube.) Slowly, they became exposed and desensitised to our world. I can't say that they suddenly lost all their morals and values, but they were willing to put them on the line to try to get this guy.

What had actually happened was this. This guy had walked up to my brother and asked if he could have a chat with him. He'd pulled him to one side, started talking to him generally about something, then pulled out a bottle and smashed it across his face. Basically, it was linked to a rave that we had gone to, in Chingford, a couple of months before.

Four or five of us had gone there, and so we'd had
all the attention in this rave. But just like it is now,
back then the feeling from the locals was, 'Who do
you think you are coming into our area, acting like
this?' It was an area thing, and there was this big
stand-off between us and them. There were loads of
them – maybe twenty, twenty-five of them, and only
five of us. But because we were confident and we
could stand our ground, we said, 'Look guys, we
haven't come in here to cause any trouble, but
we ain't going nowhere. We're staying.' So we just
went back into the rave. There was then probably a
lot of talk : 'Who are these guys? Who do they think
they are?' and so on. Then, about a month or so later,
they've clocked my brother at this fair, decided,
'That's the guy,' and some Joe has said, 'Let's get
him'. He was probably the gofer. He couldn't chuck
it himself, but with a bottle in his hand, he could
cause a lot of damage. So that's what he'd done.

All of us had been there, but my brother had stuck
out the most because he was the tallest. We knew
who the culprit was, so we talked about getting a hit
man. But all this went on the back burner because literally a few weeks later, something else happened to
our family which put this into sharp perspective.

However, it did go to court as they got the guy
who'd done it. He was only given six months of

community service – not even a prison sentence. The way they'd played it in court, it was as if Elton had been the aggressor, which of course he wasn't. But in the court there was this really little guy, standing there, and then my brother who was massive. So naturally the jury thought that this big guy must have done something to provoke the attack.

All this contributed to me losing what moral code I had left. There aren't exactly rules on the street, but I knew that there were certain things which you just did not do – picking on people who can't defend themselves, and so on. What happened to Elton changed all that, and perhaps that was why I found myself stabbing someone for their ring. I disregarded the little that remained of my values. I became slightly less human. That's the point at which my life began to turn. It wasn't that consciously I felt I needed to get somebody for what happened to my brother, but now I cared much less about the damage that I caused.

FOUR

By the age of 17, I'd got well involved in taking speed, and then more drugs to supplement that habit. This is the way that those 'softer' drugs work: speed makes you feel bigger and better than you are; hash just makes you feel dopey and drugged. But when you mix the two, you get a kind of narcotic pick-me-up. That was my life: sleeping in late over weekends because I'd been out raving, selling drugs, and going out with Sheila – and we were sleeping together now.

It was coming closer to the end of my first year of college. It was just a basic qualification, but my GCSEs weren't that good, so I had to do the first diploma as an entry to the construction diploma proper. If you get five GCSEs grade C or better then you don't have to do the first diploma, but I hadn't got the grades so I had to do it.

At that time in my life, apart from my brother's incident, things were on an even keel, steady. I wanted to get educated because I knew, realistically, that I was never going to make a career out of breaking the law. I didn't aspire to becoming a gang boss – that whole area of my life was more of a dream, or a myth that I let people believe about me. It was as if, when I wasn't studying and being a regular human being, I was living outside of reality in some sense. In line with my GCSE performance, I still wasn't a spectacular student, but I persevered with the course, I attended all the lectures and I kept up with the homework.

On the morning of 11 May 1990, my friends came around to the house. They were trying to persuade me to go to an 'acid rave', called 'The Rain Dance'. They were into acid – taking LSD to get them high and make them hallucinate. I wasn't really into it myself.

I remember my friend, Frank, coaxing me to go for about an hour. He badly wanted me to come with him – even to the point where he was going to pay the £25 for my entrance ticket. I had my own money but I hadn't been all that keen to spend so much of it on an evening I wasn't sure I'd enjoy. However, when he made that offer, I thought, *'OK, if you're going to pay for my ticket then why not?'*

I still don't really know why they wanted me to come so much. All they were saying was, 'Come on Dez, you'll have a laugh – you'll enjoy it.'

I thought we were going straight away to get the ticket but Frank said he'd have to go to his house to get the money. So instead of getting on the bus we went through the park towards his place.

That morning I'd partaken of my favourite cocktail of speed and cannabis. When I woke up each morning, I'd always have a spliff containing those two drugs – that's the way it used to work. Wake up, go to college, have a spliff on the way. Then arrive at college, have another spliff.

I wouldn't get so completely stoned that I couldn't function. I wasn't doing it just to get stoned anyway – it was more of a routine thing. Anyway, that day wasn't a college day, so I had the spliff at home with the boys. Then, after that hour of persuasion and drug consumption, Frank and I headed for the park.

We were about halfway through the park when we passed this guy. Frank made eye contact with him and, not wanting to look nervous or weak, he refused to look away. The other guy, also showing his bravado, did not look away either. Now they were both caught in a fixed gaze, and though they passed each other, they both stopped and the gazes became stares. Then, from about tenor fifteen feet apart, the two of them started shouting at each other. It was more the other guy – telling Frank to

'Go away' (in far more colourful language than that). That continued for a few moments, as the abuse got more intense and the stakes were raised.

Then, in the blink of an eye, a war of words became a war of fists and a fight kicked off. This guy started laying into Frank – battering him – and that must have gone on for a couple of minutes until Frank called an end to it.

'OK, stop!' cried Frank, wincing with pain and short on breath. 'Stop now. I've had enough.'

The guy did stop, sneering at his victory. Frank, awkward and wanting to get out of there, but still trying to hold on to his pride, turned to me and indicated that we should go.

Then he stopped. He'd forgotten to pick up his bag, which he'd dropped at the start of the fight and which was now sitting at the feet of this guy who'd just dished out a beating to him. Frank turned, and we edged forward. He motioned to the guy that he wanted to get his bag back and, surprisingly, the guy let him. Frank went across to pick up his bag, and I kept a close eye on the man.

At that moment, the fighter turned to me, and volleyed a mouthful of abuse in my direction.

'Don't talk to me like that,' I said.

As I did, he swung for me, and I ducked. As I ducked, and as he missed me, he exposed his body, and I delivered a heavy blow to his torso. He stopped in his tracks, his eyes bulging.

I stepped back, turned around and started walking away. From behind me I heard a shout, 'He's stabbed me! He's stabbed me!'

I had stabbed him. In one fluid moment, and almost without truly thinking about it, I had drawn my knife and plunged it into his body.

It was in broad daylight – it must have been about 1 o'clock in the afternoon. It was a Saturday, and a lot of people were around, but obviously not right there. I walked calmly – with the aim of not drawing attention to myself by running away. Of course, there was clearly something very wrong in the park – this man was screaming and holding his stomach, and pointing over in my direction.

I'd not noticed them before, but over the other side of the park, in the direction in which I was heading, there were these two guys who had been speaking with him a little while before the incident happened. They were his friends, and so, naturally, as they saw me walking off they came towards me.

'Oi!' said one of them, quite calmly. 'Was it you?'

'No mate,' I replied, my heart racing. 'It wasn't me.' I looked around exaggeratedly in some feeble attempt to put them off the scent. I might as well have saved my energy. I was going to need it.

They looked back at the other guy, who was pointing directly at me and shouting. There was no one else near me; no one else it could have been. Instinctively, I bolted, and they tore after me. They had their dog, running alongside, and so the four of us were all chasing one another through this busy Saturday afternoon.

Fortunately, I was quicker than them. I ran through a narrow alleyway, took a quick right, and kept running. Even the faster guy couldn't catch me and soon enough gave up. I didn't care. I just kept running and running until I had a sight of home. I was so tired – I'd been running the 400 metres and more at a sprint. I went to jump over some railings just by my house – they were only a foot high but I tripped over them because I was so shattered. As I got up, I saw there was somebody watching me. I just got up and carried on walking home.

When I went through my front door I saw my Mum there, sitting in the kitchen. She wondered why I was back so quickly, but she didn't really question me.

'Mum,' I said simply, 'I've come back.'

I went upstairs into the bathroom and locked the door. I took the knife in my hand – almost on autopilot – and turned on the tap, washing the blood from the blade and watching it swirl down the plughole. Then I walked to my bedroom and sat down, my adrenalin still pumping. On the exterior, I was managing to remain calm, perhaps because I'd not really taken into account fully what had just happened. I didn't think, with horror, *'What have I done?'* Instead, I thought that the guy shouldn't have troubled me; that'd he'd got what he deserved. That was my mindset – even after stabbing someone I was able to justify it to myself.

I heard an ambulance come down the street, and then a helicopter buzzing overhead. I didn't really think too much about it, or read much into it. *'It's standard procedure,'* I thought, although I neglected to realise that they only send a helicopter out when it's serious.

A little while after that, my friend, Frank, who I'd been with in the park called.

'Dez, what happened?' he asked. 'What have you done, man?'

'Well – you know,' I replied, slightly shakily, but holding my ground. 'He shouldn't have beaten you up. And he shouldn't have come up to my face like that.' I was still unrepentant.

I didn't face any trouble until a while after. That evening, one of the hard men of the area came and knocked on my door. He asked the same question.

'Dez, what happened?'

'This bloke got stabbed in the park,' I said. 'Why?'

'They're looking for two guys. Friends of yours, I think. Scott and Samuel – we've been driving around looking for them. Do you know where they live?'

The reason he was asking was because one of the young people who was outside the park had been asked questions. When he was asked who'd done it, he had just given those two names. This kid knew me, but didn't want to grass on me.

'He's in intensive care,' said the hard man. It still wasn't really registering with me. I was sure everything was going to be OK, and that the guy was going to live.

'You're looking for the wrong people,' I said. 'It wasn't my friends.'

And then I did something really foolish.

'It wasn't those guys,' I repeated. 'It was me. But don't say anything.'

The hard man looked at me, stunned. Then he left my doorstep, and at last it began to dawn on me that what I had done might have serious repercussions.

I didn't have long to wait.

I told my dad that evening, and he took the knife away from me. I told my mum in the morning, but perhaps because of all the incidents that had recently happened in the family, her response was quite unexpected. She didn't scream at me. She didn't wave her arms and shout. She just said this:

'You should never stab anyone in the stomach Dez. It's too dangerous. If you ever have to defend yourself again, make sure you only stab them in the arm.'

The next day – it must have again been 1 or 2 o'clock in the afternoon – there was a knock at the door. I was on the phone.

'Elton, get the door,' I shouted to my brother, who was sitting around in a string vest and boxer shorts.

I was listening to my phone call, but I kept half an ear out to hear who was at the door. This is what I heard.

'Where's your brother?' It was not a nice voice. It was a growl. Again:

'Where's your brother?' And then the words I'd never allowed myself to believe I'd hear: 'He's killed him. He's . . . killed him.'

I froze. Could it be true? Was he really dead – just from that one wound? Surely it couldn't be?

I heard the splintering of the door as these two men – and my brother and I were still just teenagers of 17 and 19 then – kicked it right in. One of them head-butted my brother to the floor, and then they both turned to look for me. They hadn't seen me yet, so I left the phone hanging in mid-air, turned and ran upstairs. I went to grab a weapon that I kept up there on top of my wardrobe – it was like a cosh stick – and as I turned to look down the stairs, I saw that my brother was on the floor, surrounded by loads of people, about fifteen men in all.

These two guys came running up the stairs towards me and I was totally outnumbered.

'Alright,' I said, offering myself to them in the hope they'd go easy. 'Alright.'

'Get him down the stairs!' screamed someone, along with a string of swear words.

The two men threw me down the stairs, and everyone started laying into me and my brother, stamping, kicking and punching at us viciously. Half way through this, I realised that my younger brother was sitting in the front room. I had to try to protect him, even though I was being attacked from all sides. So I shot up out of the curled ball I'd become on the floor and shouted his name at the top of my voice. Further blows rained down on me after that, but about twenty seconds later, the woman from across the road came out of her door, saw what was going on, and started screaming. She'd been cutting up some vegetables for dinner, and she'd heard all the commotion from across the road.

When she saw the devastation at our front door, she screamed at these men:

'Stop! Stop! You'll kill them, you'll kill them!'

It was broad daylight, and these men realised that they'd been clocked and ran off. The woman came across and was horrified at what she saw. There was glass and blood everywhere. She took Jamie, our younger brother who had come out crying, across the road to look after until our parents returned. So then it was just Elton and me alone. We looked at one another and, with the blood still running down our faces, both our minds turned instinctively to revenge. For a moment, we talked about going to the pub where we knew they'd be. We even got knives, and prepared to go over there. But thankfully, we decided that that would be stupid.

Instead, we rang my dad, and brought total chaos into his day.

'Look, Dad,' I can still remember saying. 'It's kicked off. Me and Elton have taken a kicking. They said that the guy is dead. You need to come home.'

Both our parents came home from work quickly, and a little while after that my cousins and an aunt and uncle came, too. I guess the family was just rallying round together, although I was too spaced by all that had gone on to realise that was what was happening. An hour after that, my parents called a friend to come round and start fixing the windows and the door, and about an hour after that the police knocked. There were two policemen standing at the still-splintered door, with a meat wagon packed with quite a few officers and a couple of CID as well. Incredibly, even at this moment I still hadn't quite realised the enormity of what had happened – as if I couldn't actually process the fact that the guy was dead.

'Is Dez Brown there?' asked one of them.

'He's here,' said my parents, as I trudged into view.

'We're arresting you for murder.'

I didn't break down. I didn't cry. Obviously now I realised – as my rights were read to me – that this was serious; that I really had ended someone's life. I don't think that emotionally I was out of control – just quiet. My parents held it together too – they took me upstairs, told me they'd always be with me, and helped me to gather the clothes I'd been wearing when the incident happened. Then we went outside. My dad took out the knife and handed it over, and the policemen asked me to step into the van.

FIVE

I was to spend that night in the police station, but I did get to take a little trip. Seeing the state that I'd been left in by my fifteen assailants, the police had to take me to hospital. I walked along in handcuffs, with officers on all sides of me. I could feel hundreds of pairs of eyes looking at me as I went. Everyone in the hospital wondered who this boy was, with all these policemen and cuts and bruises all over him. All the skin on my back was gone from the stamping, and there were great cuts on my legs that looked like they needed stitches. In fact they never even took my handcuffs off – the doctor just looked at me and said, 'You'll be alright.' The hospital staff wiped up a few areas and that was it.

I was taken back to the police station and kept under 24-hour surveillance. Police officers sat outside the open cell doors – apparently they had to make sure that I didn't try to commit suicide. A few members of the family came up and visited me there in the police station. They didn't really ask me what had happened, just how I felt and whether I was OK.

The police had to cross-examine me, so I was there for a day and a half, and then they moved me to Brixton Prison. In Brixton, I was banged up with a guy who'd recently broken into Cilla Black's house. The first day I was there, he was telling me about all these places that he had burgled, and I immediately relaxed. This was entertaining! And that's the kind of vibe that you get in prison, because you know everyone wants to know what you are in there for. If you're banged up with someone you don't know, you get to know them. I was assigned to F-wing – they called it 'Fraggle Rock'. In Brixton Prison, the two worst wings are A-Wing and F-Wing. A-Wing is for the IRA and really notorious criminals – people who are seen as a real danger. There's a massive electric door to get into it, and while F-Wing is obviously high-security, it's the next level down. I was to be the youngest on the wing.

The first day I arrived I saw some friends from the street who were already there.

'Dez,' one of them said, surprised to see me. 'How come you're in here?'

I told them what had happened.

'We heard all about that,' he said, looking slightly shocked that it was me who had done it.

Straight away I got respect from the other inmates because of my offence. The fact that I had killed somebody, made me someone. I don't mean that it made me feel at home, but it did make me feel that I was not there on my own. I was with other people that I knew, and who respected me. I went on to my wing for the first time, and the screws (prison officers) told me that I had to put on a uniform.

'You're joking,' I said, arrogantly. 'I'm not wearing that.'

These clothes were rubbish, I thought to myself, and there was no way that I was putting them on. So even here, detained by the law at 17 for what could be murder, I was still showing a remarkable amount of front. So when they weren't looking, I ditched these clothes and managed to keep my own on. At least, most of the time – because when you go to prison, they strip you naked to make sure you're not hiding anything. That was a scary experience. I'm standing there, naked as the day I was born, and there are screws pointing and laughing and making sarcastic comments.

'Don't be shy, son,' joked one of them. I certainly was shy. I'd never been in that situation before and so I was worried about what was going on. At that moment, prison did not seem like a comfortable place.

On my arrival in F-Wing, I saw this massive black guy there who called me over.

'What are you in here for, mate?' he asked.

'I'm in here for murder.' I replied, without flinching.

'Yeah,' he said, smiling. 'Respect. Respect.'

That was the attitude of the people in there. This guy was massive, and yet he respected me for killing someone.

I chatted to my room-mate, who also showed me respect, despite my age. He was saying that he was what they call 'code E' and that he was in there for beating up an elderly woman. I remembered that the case had been in the paper – the woman involved was really old, and it was a horrible crime. But he told me that he hadn't done it and that he knew who had. Now he was going to make sure that the guy who'd really done it, who was also on F-Wing now, would get what they call 'nonced off'. If someone has either raped or attacked an old woman, they get 'nonced off', which means they get made fun of constantly, slapped and even totally battered by the other inmates because it's seen as a degrading offence.

The next morning, I got out of my cell first thing. Outside there was this guy, whose hair was just wild. He was an African man, with wild hair, and really white eyes that were just the same. I walked on, a little freaked out, and talked to some of the other prisoners. Someone told me that there was a guy on A-Wing who'd put his wife in a great big tub of acid. That freaked me out some more. Going in there, I'd thought my offence was serious, but meeting some of these characters put it into some kind of warped perspective.

My week in Brixton was a blur of experiences that came so fast that I couldn't process them properly. I was so green and so new to all this, I could scarcely take it all in. I saw a guy across the wing who they called 'animal' – because he was tattooed almost from head to toe. He'd been in there for eleven years. In the middle of the night, when I couldn't sleep, I'd hear other people screaming out at 2 o'clock in the morning, followed by screws running in there and injecting them with Valium to calm them down. There were no toilets in our cells, and no TVs. Nowadays you get a toilet and a TV and everything else; back then there were just buckets. I didn't have a shower for the whole week, scared by the stories I'd heard on the wing. I barely ate either, because I'd heard that people urinated in the food. Though being a killer gained me respect, I never felt anything approaching safe.

I told the prison psychiatrist that I needed to get transferred out of there. 'This is an adult prison,' I said. 'I'm on F-Wing and I'm 17 years old – surely that can't be right?' Thankfully, the prison authorities agreed, and they did move me, to Feltham.

I was in Feltham for four weeks, and almost as soon as I arrived I went to a Magistrates' Court to see if I could get bail. (It's more of a routine formality than a cast-iron hope. It's an option you have, so you always go for it.) They turned me down, as could be expected on a murder charge, and so I returned to Feltham.

The way that Feltham worked at that time was that it was very much a black and white culture, further divided by the sort of area you came from: either the North, West, South or East of London, or specific areas within them. Because I came from Essex – which they call East London – I could only really make alliances with other guys who were from that part of the world. But one alliance I made in there came about very differently. There was this big guy in the prison called Steam. He could push nearly 170 kilos and he was only 20 years old – he was massive. We were in a shower one time after gym. Steam and this guy they called Ragga were there. They were widely regarded as the two hard men of the prison. I was in there using my shower gel and Steam just grabbed it out of my hand and started using it. Without thinking, I shouted, 'What do you think you're doing?'

Steam and Ragga looked at each other.

'Who are you talking to?' asked Steam, incredulous that someone would dare speak to him in this way. He squeezed out a great handful of my shower gel, and then just flung the bottle out.

'What are you doing?' I asked again. I stepped out of the shower, picked up the bottle, and came back into the shower to finish off.

'Right,' growled Ragga. 'We'll deal with you later.'

I didn't let my fear show, but I wasn't stupid. I was no weight at all compared to them; I was really skinny and Steam was huge. Still, the way I looked at it, a fight was now going to happen, and while I was a little bit shaken up, I just thought that whether we stabbed one another or bit one another, no matter what it was, I just had to go for it. It wouldn't happen then and there – fights like that were arranged, they didn't just happen – so I knew I'd have to wait for the call.

Later on, when most of the wing were watching a video, he signalled to me that it was time to go and fight. I stood to my feet to follow him, but one of the screws clocked me.

'Where are you going Brown?' he barked. 'Sit down – you're not going anywhere.'

There was nothing I could do. I looked across at Steam, almost apologetically, and sat down. There was nothing I could do once the screw had seen us make the move. The fight was off, and though my relief was mixed with a strange disappointment, I still wonder quite what that screw spared me from.

The following day, as we were queuing up for dinner, Steam sidled up to me. For some reason, the following words came out of my mouth:

'Look Steam, if you had just asked me for some shower gel I would have given it to you. But to just grab it out of my hand like that is not on.' Phew, that was pretty brave.

'Look,' he said, 'I respect you for standing up to me like that. We're quits – forget it.'

'*RESULT!*' I thought. Straight away I had earned the respect of one of the top guys in Feltham – the hardest man there. And I didn't even have to fight him to get it.

Sheila came to visit me in Feltham. There was something different about her when she arrived. I couldn't put my finger on it, though, at least until she spoke . . .

'Dez,' she said, with unexpected emotion, 'I've been saved.'

I gave her a sideways look to indicate that I didn't have a clue what she was talking about. 'Saved?' I replied. 'Saved from what?'

'I've become a Christian,' she said.

I laughed at her. I wasn't interested in that because in my own mind I was my own god. I decided what was right and what was wrong.

Of course, that wasn't the first time in my life that the subject of God had been broached. Before I went inside, my sister, who was no Christian, said to me, 'Make sure you read your Bible and pray, Dez.' Why she said that to me, I don't know.

And the funny thing is this – when I was in prison, I used to do just that. I didn't so much read my Bible, but I used to pray quite a lot. I had this routine for myself each night. I'd do my secret roll-up, and put it on the side. Then I'd do my weights, which consisted of me bench-pressing the bed, and then I'd get up and smoke the cigarette. After that, I'd get into my bed and I'd pray. That was it; that was my routine.

'God,' I'd say. 'Look after my family and please look after Sheila. Help me while I'm in here.' I even used to ask God to forgive me for what I had done – but it wasn't because I was totally repentant. More that I felt what I'd done was an accident which I hadn't really meant to happen.

Where it came from I don't know. I would sit down and close my eyes. Then I used to put my hands together and pray. Sometimes I used to pray for five or ten minutes, just speaking out all these different things, asking for help for my family, help for my brother, help for so-and-so.

I'd been put on one of the roughest wings in Feltham at that time. Literally every other day the alarms would go off because fighting had broken out. When there was a fight, people would chuck tea in other people's faces and whack chairs over their heads – and that was every other day. So, despite my close shave with Steam, I guess it was only natural that I'd end up in a fight myself.

It just started as a bit of 'cussing' in the pool room. Me and this other guy were dishing out verbal abuse to one another, about image or girls or whatever. But he got serious and took it to another level, cussing my mum. Naturally enough, I cussed his mum, and everyone around us started laughing, because to them it was like television – their day's entertainment. He couldn't take the fact that people were laughing about his mum, so he walked across to where I was sitting and spat at me. That was too much for me and I squared up to him. We couldn't fight then and there, with screws around, so we arranged to fight in the showers.

A few people had come down to watch and, unfortunately for me, they were all his friends. The fight kicked off and he punched me, so I threw him on to the floor. But as I went to kick him in the head and start laying into him properly, these guys who were friends of his jumped in.

'Stop!' they shouted. 'Stop! The screws are coming.'

Actually, the screws weren't coming but the fight was over. I had a shower, and he went back into the pool room. My nose was bleeding from the one punch he'd landed, and because of that, he thought that he'd gained the upper hand. That really got to me.

There's this thing we used to do, back on the street, that's hard to explain to those who weren't in on it. There was this kind of 'mental mode' which we used to go into for a joke. It's like this really careless attitude, where you just act slightly mad, but not completely mad. So when I went into the pool room and he was with all his friends, I went into this mode. I was just laughing and staring, a bit maniacally, and that obviously annoyed him.

'Why are you staring at me?' he shouted, clearly rattled. 'What are you laughing at?'

The screws, who could see what was going on through the window in their office, were laughing at him. Still, I laughed and stared. He came over and bounced this snooker ball on the floor so it bounced up, just missing my face. He couldn't take a swing at me because there were screws watching, so we just pushed one another a little. Nothing came of that there and then, but walking back to the cells, I realised that people were beginning to gang up on me because this guy had been in the prison for a long time and was well known.

I started to plan how I could get him but I knew that I had to go to court. If I turned up in court with any bruises on my face it wouldn't reflect well on me.

In fact, after being enemies with this guy for a short time, and fighting with him, he was the one to call a truce. He came to me and said that he had got hold of some drugs – some weed. I just had to give him some of my canteen, he told me, and he would fix me up. Now, wisdom, I thought, says that it's better to be friends with someone than to be enemies with him and his friends – ten or fifteen of them. Especially if you are going to be in for a long time. So I agreed, and when I came out for 'association' – which is kind of prison break-time – I gave him some of my canteen: a bottle of drink, biscuits and some crisps. In prison, your canteen is your currency, and association is an important time because it gives you somewhere to meet. We did meet, and I handed over my currency – my drink, biscuits and crisps – to him. He told me that when he got back to his cell he'd send down the drugs for me.

I also returned to my cell, and waited excitedly for the package from my new ally. Right on time, the package arrived as promised – a little matchbox that I hoped would be packed with enough drugs to last me a good while. Making sure there were no screws around, I slid the box open . . . and saw human faeces inside!

It seemed as if everyone in the prison started laughing at that point. I sat in my cell and boiled with rage and embarrassment. 'That's it,' I said quietly to myself. 'This is war. I'm going to get him for this. I'm going to batter him.'

But again, I knew that I had to go to court in a few days' time. I didn't think I was going to get bail, so I decided to go to court, at least look presentable, and then when I returned, tear him apart.

For the next few days, I devoted my time to meditating on how I was going to get this guy. I planned to get him back – really get him. That he had sent faeces to my cell had completely embarrassed me and destroyed the image I'd built up. He needed to pay for that damage. Even when I left for court, I was spitting fire at the other prisoners, telling them all how I was 'going to get him'.

I went to the Magistrates' Court. The way the judicial system worked back then meant that you'd get three attempts at bail. Two of them would be at the Magistrates' Court, and then one would be at Crown Court. If you were ever going to get bail on a charge like mine, you were only going to get it at Crown Court. I knew that: that was the conventional wisdom; it was what everybody told me. Man, I wanted to hurt that guy for his little matchbox trick.

I never got a chance to finish that war as they gave me bail at the Magistrates' Court. For £25,000, security money that my parents had to pledge, I was allowed back into the outside world. If I were to abscond or go missing, my parents would have to pay the £25,000 – they'd have had to sell their house to raise that amount. That was a big step for my parents; they were already in the process of buying another house because of the hostility in the area that was now piled up against my family. By then, anyone associated with me was regularly getting beaten up.

My parents' lives, at that moment in time, were in total disarray. To make matters worse, this was the early 1990s, when the UK economy had gone into recession and the housing market had gone sour. They couldn't live in their old area any longer because of the stigma that I had brought, but they couldn't sell their house either. Interest rates were up at around 11 per cent, and that meant that no one wanted to buy a house.

My parents had to go to the bank manager cap-in-hand, asking him to help. Somehow – my father said he was the best bank manager ever – he found a way, and gave them an extra loan so that they could buy another house. Of course, they still had a big mortgage left on their first house but they could rent it out. Still, with my bail money included, they found themselves in debt to the tune of more than £100,000.

I had to move to a new address – my aunt's place in the country part of Essex. That location wasn't disclosed in court, so that friends or family of the deceased wouldn't be able to trace me. I was shocked that I'd got bail. Instead of returning to Feltham, as I'd fully expected, I was in many senses a free man again.

When I came out I got to read all the letters that had been sent to me while I'd been inside. I had one letter that stood out from the rest. It was from a couple who'd lived a road up from where I lived when the incident happened. They were Christians.

I'd never thought about it much at the time – to me they'd always just been those parents who were very strict with their son and never let him come out because he had to go to church or do his homework. I'd never really known his mum and dad, except to say hello to. But here was a letter from them, and it said:

'We're praying for you Dez. God can help you in this situation. Trust in him. Blah blah blah.'

Normally, I would have dismissed this but for some reason it all felt quite significant. My girlfriend had become a Christian and kept trying to tell me about God. My sister, who wasn't even a Christian, had told me I should read the Bible and pray. And now this letter – out of the blue. For a while, this kind of religious vibe came over me, but again I decided that I wasn't interested. God just wasn't something that I understood, and I couldn't see how religion was going to help me.

SIX

When I came out on bail, I had to move to my 'aunt's' house, although this lady wasn't actually my biological aunt. She grew up near Mum and they were very good friends. When I was a child, she was always the person who would look after us when Mum couldn't. She'd said that I could move in with her while I was on bail, as it was more likely that out in her corner of Essex I'd be able to stay out of trouble. And it made a lot of sense – she was like a second mum to me.

Every day, I used to have to sign on at the local police station. It was one of the conditions of my bail: I had to travel to the station once in the morning and once in the evening every day, just to show my face, and to prove that I was still where I said I was and that I hadn't fled the country. That was how it was for the first couple of months. After they passed without problems, the visits dropped down to once a day. Then it got down to about twice a week.

Alongside that restriction to my lifestyle, there were also various areas of London and Essex that I wasn't allowed to visit or travel through. Although I managed to sign on each day, I did bend the second restriction several times, going through areas that I was banned from. It was only to visit friends, and I was only passing through but, strictly speaking, I was breaking the rules.

I'd been fortunate to get bail, and even more fortunate to somehow get it at the Magistrates' Court. When I left the court, the one thing that everyone from the judge to my parents advised me to do sounded simple enough: stay out of trouble. But I was Dez Brown. And that just wasn't me.

There was this guy who took a liking to Sheila, my girlfriend. I'd spoken to him on the phone, and he'd run his mouth off at me. Eventually, wound up by his words, I asked him to come down and see me.

He did come down, to Walthamstow, the area where Sheila lived, but he'd brought friends, and he clearly intended to have a fight with me. I was used to these kinds of odds from prison, and I was growing to like them less and less. Once again, it was just me, my enemy and his mates. So he came down to Sheila's, knocked on the door of her flat and set his mouth off into overdrive again.

'Look,' I said, interrupting the constant stream of swear words. 'Just get lost.'

'No,' he replied, aware of how he and his mates outnumbered me. 'Let's fight instead.'

'What's the point in that? There's three of you and only one of me.'

'They won't come down. It'll just be you and me.'

'*I'm not stupid*,' I thought. '*I'm not some kind of hero*.' There was no way that, in my right mind, I was going to get into a fight while I still had to sign on twice a week with the police.

'No – forget that.' I replied, and hoped it would stop there.

Of course, it didn't stop there. He started saying things about Sheila, and some pretty serious cusses about me, and eventually he achieved his objective and wound me up sufficiently.

'Alright,' I snapped. 'We'll do it.'

I went back into the house for a minute and saw Sheila, who was begging me not to go and fight. I insisted – and anyway I'd psyched myself up into fight mode by then. Realising she couldn't talk me out of it, she instead reached for something in her kitchen drawer.

'Here,' she said, 'take this'.

She handed me a knife. And it wasn't a little flick knife – it was a big kitchen knife, about six inches long. I stood there, in what was perhaps a life-defining moment and weighed up the situation. If I went out unarmed, I could get into real trouble if the fight turned nasty. But then, looking at that knife, I realised that if I took it, I'd end up using it. If I did that, I knew that that was my life ruined, and that'd be me disappearing down the prison plughole for a long stretch.

'No,' I said. 'I can't take it.'

I'll never know how important that decision was.

We walked down to the street level, to an appropriate fighting place and, as promised, his friends stayed away. A fight kicked off between us and, in street terms, I battered this guy. It came to the point when I'd got him on the floor and was just holding him saying, 'Give up, it's finished.' Just then, his two friends decided to break their promise and began to advance towards me. As they did, the one on the floor stabbed me with his knife, once in the top of the leg and once in the backside.

I went ballistic. Sheila, terrified that I'd was bleeding now from a stab wound of my own, called a man that she knew nearby and a over and bring order to what nasty.

Calmly, and holding my up to the guy who had though he was still stan went right up to his face. It was also covered in blood.

'You're finished,' I said, dramatically. 'You're finished.'

He was shaking. I don't think he could quite believe that he'd stabbed me and, even more, he and his friends were shocked that I had not run off when I had the chance. I was still shouting and arguing with them, even with two holes in me.

For days following that, friends of mine would come around to see me, just to make sure that I was OK after this second incident. We had cannabis-smoking sessions at the end of the garden – we were a bit more discreet than we used to be. We used to be up there for hours. My brother would be there, too, just smoking and chilling out.

We spent ages talking, and eventually somebody suggested that we get this guy who'd stabbed me. My best friend knew somebody who had a gun, and it would cost about £80 to get hold of it.

get the gun, find out where this
m.' The way I saw it, with my
s a kind of extended self-
d stabbed me first. Because
d the brief experience I'd
ought I could handle

something like this. Anyway, I wasn't intending to shoot him dead, probably just fire a couple of rounds in his legs, to do him a bit of permanent damage.

But I didn't get hold of the gun, and I didn't go in search of revenge. Instead, I just had this weird feeling that I couldn't shake. Somehow, although my head told me I'd been wronged and needed to get even, something else was telling me to stop.

Back to that day though. I returned to Sheila's flat and called a cab. The car arrived and I didn't say anything to the driver, except, 'Whipps Cross Hospital, please.' I just sat there in the cab, as the whole seat got more and more saturated with my blood.

At the hospital, it soon became apparent that I'd have to have stitches. This was bad news. It meant that I wouldn't be able to get home on time, and therefore I'd be too late to sign on at the police station as I was supposed to that night. And that meant that I had broken my bail conditions.

As soon as I'd been stitched up, I knew I had to ring my parents and let them know what had happened. They were surprisingly composed right then, but I wasn't prepared for the reaction that was to come a little later from them.

I finally got home just after 11 p.m. I had been due at the police station between 8 and 9 p.m., and when I did finally get there, around 10 p.m., I lied to the duty police officer, telling him that I'd been stuck on a delayed train. Because it was the first time I'd been late, they let me off with a warning, as long as I saw to it that it didn't happen again. '*I've got away with that*,' I thought, breathing a deep sigh of relief.

Strangely, considering what had gone before, my walk home brought some brief peace. I had to go through the countryside to get to my parents' house, and at that time of night it was all very quiet and still.

I got home, still full of relief at my lucky escape, and a lot more peaceful than I had been after the fight. Inside, I saw my mum and dad. They weren't as pleased to see me as I'd hoped. In fact they were crying – something I'd never seen my father do before. My brother was also crying.

'Dez,' he exclaimed. 'What are you doing to the family? You are destroying it!'

I looked across at my mum, who was also sobbing. 'You're just completely off the rails, son,' she said, with tears running down her face.

Prison hadn't changed me much. All the fighting had hardened me up further. Despite all the trouble

I was in, I still drank, I still smoked, I still took plenty of drugs. Through it all, I was still my own god, I felt like I was in control, and nothing in the world was going to convince me otherwise. But coming home that night, seeing my parents crying like that, and really hearing and feeling their disappointment where before I'd allowed it to bounce off me – well, I think that was the point at which I finally began to realise that my life was out of control, because it was having such an effect on those close to me.

It was shortly after that that Sheila persuaded me to go to what she called her 'church house group'. I didn't know what to expect from that title. Did they sit around talking about boring, weird God stuff that I wouldn't understand? Apparently not. Instead, there were all these young people sitting around. They were pleased to see me, and what was weird was that they told me that they'd all been praying for me for the last few weeks, even though they didn't know me.

The following Sunday, I went along with Sheila to a church in Walthamstow. It wasn't her church, but there was this crazy Jamaican preacher who was speaking there, and she wanted to go along. There was a strange atmosphere, unlike anything I'd ever experienced before. Some of the people were falling down, apparently under the power of God. Also, it seemed that people were getting healed of illnesses and physical problems. It was mad.

I remember the preacher standing at the front and saying to the congregation, 'If you've done wrong in your life, come up here to the front of the church.'

I looked around. If anyone in that place had done wrong, it was me. So, suddenly, there I am, in a church, walking up to the front with trousers rolled up, hair in twists and a bandana on top. Very quickly, all these people came around me. One of them spoke to me, 'Do you want to ask God to forgive you?' she asked.

'Yeah,' I said, speaking as I thought. 'I do.'

They talked me through this prayer, the basic content of which was saying, 'God forgive him.' As they prayed, I felt like a weight was being lifted from my shoulders. I actually felt good.

Then one of the others asked me if I'd like to be filled with the Holy Spirit? I really didn't know what that meant, but my attitude right in that moment was that God was proving to be good, and if the Holy Spirit was more of God, then it sounded alright to me.

Very quickly, I prayed out loud myself, just throwing out words to God – nothing poetic, just what came out. After about ten seconds, I realised that I wasn't speaking in English. It was no language I recognised either – just this strange, unknown dialect. I hadn't disengaged my brain, but these foreign words were pouring out of me, and I started to think to myself, *'Dez what are you doing? You're talking gobbledegook!'* It was only later that I discovered I had been doing what they call 'speaking in tongues' – that is, talking in a divinely-inspired language.

I stopped, turned around and sat down. For a while I just sat there, thinking, *'Whoa!'* Something significant had happened to me. I didn't know what it was, but I definitely felt different.

I left that place feeling like I was walking on air.

I returned, excited, to the church the following week, but inside I found no Jamaican preacher, no miracle healings, and no people speaking in a divine tongue. Instead, the church just seemed to have died. All I was looking for at that time in my life was what I could get, and I badly wanted the same kind of emotional uplift that the church had given me the previous weekend. With all the negative things going on in and around my life, all I wanted was to feel good. The first time, the church had given me that – now it looked like it wasn't going to be repeated. I thought that that might be the end of the road for church and me. But, about a fortnight later, Sheila invited me to come to her church. It was a completely different kind of church, very traditional. The women there were all wearing hats and long skirts, and most of the men were in smart suits. And then there was me, with my trousers rolled up and my bandana, turning up at this church and drawing quite a bit of attention to myself.

There were lot of people there who Sheila knew and who I didn't, and also a lot of young people – it just so happened that a lot of them had become Christians there. For instance, one girl there had been kidnapped when she was younger and taken to Egypt because her dad was a very rich Muslim. She escaped and found God while living on the streets. Then there was another guy who'd been in prison for armed robbery and he'd become a Christian, too. There was Sheila's brother who had been on drugs and, because of his dyslexia, could neither read nor write. Yet when he became a Christian, God helped him to begin to read the Bible.

So there were all these people I kind of identified with, who'd known violence, or spent time inside, or had been on drugs. They made up this church, where I was again hearing the message of Jesus, and so I felt like I fitted in there, despite my different clothes. As I listened, I didn't really understand all of what was being said, but I did hear, once again, those same kind of words. 'If you have done wrong in your life and you want God to forgive you, come up to the front.'

Well, that was me. So I walked up to the front, again I prayed the prayer, asking that God would forgive the wrong I'd done. I prayed with someone there that God would help me to live a different kind of life.

At this church, the people asked me to come to the room at the back. They wanted to take down my details so that they could follow up the commitment I'd made that morning. When I got back there, I was confronted by this large woman, jumping up and down and crying!

'Dez,' she sobbed, 'we've been praying for you!'

For the first time in my life, the love of God hit me between the eyes. Not through anything supernatural – or through a touch from God himself – but because, no matter how much I tried to project this hard, rude boy exterior, I was so struck by this woman that I almost cried myself. She didn't know me but, like many others, she knew about me and the terrible thing that I had done. And yet she was crying for me, and that touched me.

I did give them my details, and as I did so I felt this amazing sense of belonging. Along with that came two very alien desires. I wanted to read the Bible – even though I'd barely touched it before – and I wanted to pray.

I got a Bible for my birthday, the Good News version with little stick man illustrations in it. I'd read it whenever I could – sometimes until 12 or 1 o'clock in the morning. No one else in my house was a Christian, so I'd hole myself up in my room and just read for hours at a time. My dad had flirted with Christianity about twenty-five years earlier, but apart from that no one else in my family had a sense of God.

One night, I felt that God himself was speaking to me. It's a little hard to explain how I knew that – I was just reading the Gospel of Matthew, and suddenly the words seemed to lift off the page and speak directly into my life. The passage was Matthew chapter 9, verse 6 – a scene where a man who is totally paralysed is brought before Jesus. Jesus acknowledges the faith of this man's friends who went to extraordinary lengths to get him there, lowering him through the roof of the building where he was. Then Jesus says to the man, 'Son, your sins are forgiven; take up your bed and go home.' At that moment, I felt God say to me –

almost in an audible voice – 'Dez, I have forgiven you of your sins. You're not going to prison, you're going home.'

Now for someone who had done as much as I had, and been through everything that I had been through, that was a big statement. It was mad in fact. But at the same time, I knew that God had spoken to me. I didn't understand it, but I knew it was true. God told me this, and he gave me the faith to believe it.

It was late at night, and after spending some more time in prayer, I fell asleep. The next morning, when I woke up, I rushed down to see my mum and dad to tell them what had happened. I told my barrister. I told my solicitor. I even told my friends. 'I'm not going back into prison – God has spoken to me.'

The church that I belonged to possibly wasn't ready for this. They'd always preached this stuff – God speaks and he can make the impossible happen – but suddenly they had a dilemma. Should they believe this criminal who was saying that God had spoken to him and told him he was not going to prison, when that seemed so very far-fetched? Or, should they look at the odds and think, in reality, that it could never happen? They took the more difficult option, and supported me. They decided to put their prayers behind what I'd said, believing that God, who can make all things possible, had truly chosen to intervene in my life.

Since I'd moved area, I hadn't had a lot of contact with my old street friends. But just at that time, I did run into a group of them, and I told them what God had said to me.

'Well,' I remember one of them saying, 'either there is a God, or you're mad.'

They must have been thinking, *'This guy has got religious mania. He's tipped off the scale! Eight weeks ago he was out there robbing people – now he's telling me that I need to ask God's forgiveness for the wrongs that I've done!'*

I didn't have religious mania. I'd realised that I could have a relationship with Jesus Christ. And even now, while on bail for murder, I felt an amazing inner peace that I'd never experienced in my life before.

A while after that, again I found myself asking God for forgiveness; at that time not understanding that I'd already been forgiven completely by him. I was in my house, on my own, praying, 'God forgive me! God forgive me!'

Out of the blue, what I can only describe as a 'presence' just hit my body and I began to sob. Through everything that had gone on, I hadn't shed any tears, even lying awake at night in a cold prison cell with a bucket for a toilet. But now, in this moment, alone in my room, I felt a wave of emotion, and then the tears came. As they did, I just began to say those words over and over again – 'God forgive me! God forgive me!' And these weren't regular tears, with them came something else. I felt a huge release. Before, as much as I had believed that God had forgiven me, now I *knew* that he had. It was no longer only based on what I thought, but also what I felt. All the emotion, tension and frustration that was stored up inside me was released.

And something had changed. I walked around the house, and slightly different words came out: 'God has forgiven me. God has forgiven me.'

I no longer felt like there was a huge debt that had to be paid. Of course, I couldn't argue theologically that Jesus had in some way paid that debt for me, but I knew that I had been forgiven. So there I was, knowing that I had been forgiven. God himself had spoken to me, and my life had completely changed direction. I knew that I could no longer live life for myself – but for him.

Meeting the younger group of people at church helped me a lot. They were around my own age and shared some of my background, so they gave me a sense of belonging. I had become a Christian and, rather than immediately having to spend all my time with people who knew nothing of the kind of life I had lived and the things I had been through, I was able to identify with other Christians who had come from a more streetwise, urban context. They'd all been through drugs, they'd all been through sexual promiscuity, and many of them had also been through raving. What really challenged me was that these people who had once lived in those ways were now completely changed and completely passionate about God. It kind of rubbed off on me. There was a really positive vibe among us, and a shared passion which we'd encourage each other to keep up. We were almost competitive in a healthy way – spurring each other on to do more and more for God.

So when somebody in the group told us about how they'd met someone in the street and told them about Jesus, the rest of us would want to go and find someone else in the street and tell them about him, too. If you heard others talking about how somebody had been spiritually healed, the rest of us would want to go and pray for somebody to see if they got healed as well. Being around each other, egging one another on, released our expectations of what God could do – and sure enough, he didn't disappoint us. Although, compared to many other Christians, we were possibly living in quite a radical way, we didn't see ourselves like that. Instead, we just thought that that was what Christianity was like.

A woman who I didn't know came up to me in church. She opened her purse, pulled out a £10 note, and gave it to me. 'Buy yourself a shirt,' she said, with a smile.

Our church was quite traditional, and the kind of clothes that me and the other young people wore weren't exactly in keeping with the rest of the church's clothing. If this lady had come up to me and said that a few weeks earlier, I probably would have been rude to her and never darkened the doors of the place again. But instead I thought, '*Thank God! If this can help me better myself as a Christian, and demonstrate my respect for God, then yes, I will go and do it.*' In fact, I went out and bought a few shirts. I later came to understand that God wanted my heart, not my clothes.

Our group belonged and helped each other, and really just wanted to live for God. We were a community, jam-packed with enthusiasm, if perhaps lacking in wisdom.

Sheila was over the moon that I had become a Christian. As it was, her brother, her brother's friends and even her friends had become Christians – and now I, too, had made that decision. It was incredible – like a miniature spiritual revival in East London. From a Christian perspective, she was really excited that I'd chosen to follow that path, and from a human perspective, I think she at last began to feel that she didn't have to worry about me any more.

SEVEN

One night a friend came over to see me. I was still out in the Essex countryside at that time. It was a bit of a journey for him, a little more than an hour, and after it got late we decided he should stay the night. At about 2 o'clock in the morning there was banging on the door.

I was a Christian then but these were the early stages of my faith and I was spending time with some of my old friends. I was still seeing drugs and all kinds of things like that but, with God's help trying not to get involved with them.

We looked out of the window and realised that the whole house was surrounded by police. I looked out to the back garden and saw policemen with dogs, meat wagons and the whole thing. My heart was pumping in my chest. I was going straight! Surely they weren't going to try and pin something on me now?

There were about twenty of them in all, and we were completely surrounded. So I went downstairs to find my parents who were already up. My dad trudged to the door, wondering what on earth I'd done this time.

'Is Elton Brown there?' asked a policeman. 'I've come to arrest him.'

It wasn't me they wanted – it was my brother! And what's more, they'd sent twenty police round to get him at 2 o'clock in the morning. My friend, who knew what I'd done and could now see the whole house surrounded, must have been wondering what I was involved in here. At the same time, I was desperately trying to work out what Elton had done that would warrant this.

My brother was bundled into a van, and soon afterwards I found out that he had been doing street robberies on people that sell flowers along A-roads. He would drive up to one, stop the car, and with a friend pull out a knife demanding the flower-seller's money. Then they'd get back into the car, drive further on to the next one, and rob him, too. They had been doing this like plums though – complete amateurs. They'd made no attempt to cover their number plate, and so when they drove off from one of the robberies, the man who'd been robbed just called the police with the registration number. And obviously Elton's friend wasn't quite the most honourable man in the world; as soon as the police caught up with him he just grassed on my brother and blamed it all on him.

Finally, they'd come looking for Elton. But knowing that a murderer on bail lived in the same house, they thought it best to send a small army to go and get him. Which explained why the house had been surrounded like some kind of hostage siege.

So my family had their next nightmare. Already they had one son who was facing the courts for murder; now their other son was being arrested for street robbery with a knife. That was also a very serious charge – it isn't like going up to someone and saying, 'Give us your money!' It's regarded as threatening to stab them – robbery with intent.

My own court hearing eventually came around and was due to last for two weeks. By that time, I had been reading and praying a lot, and also fasting – denying myself food as an act of worship. I can genuinely say that I was a Christian, off drugs, still dealing with issues of sex, but genuinely on track and just wanting to serve God. I had managed to acquire a job working in a barber's shop, from a Christian woman who owned a hair salon. I hadn't gone back to college after being let out on bail – there were too many old connections there.

For the hearing, I had to travel down to the Old Bailey every day with Mum, Dad and Sheila. When I arrived there, though, I saw many of my friends were there to support me. It must have been very hostile for them as the deceased's family and friends were also there, but still they came, and continued to come each day.

I had met my barrister only once in the whole time leading up to the trial, and that was only for about twenty minutes. '*Surely this guy can't defend me?*' I thought. '*I've spent less than half an hour with him.*' And in that time, he'd barely spoken about the case; he just told me how to present myself – to dress in a plain shirt and tie, and cut my hair.

I didn't have to speak on the first day of the trial, because at first they were bringing in witnesses. Then, when a friend of the deceased was cross-examined, he became very agitated by the process. Understandably, he was wondering why he was receiving such a hostile approach, when I, the killer, was sitting peacefully in another part of the courtroom.

The man whose life I had taken had been a soldier with the British Army and had done time in Northern Ireland. His dad was a high-ranking policeman who worked at Scotland Yard. So, in many ways, I felt that the system was definitely going to be in their favour, rather than mine.

One of the character witnesses who spoke for me was my pastor, who explained about my conversion to Christianity and the big changes in my personality. There was a sigh in the court as she said that – people thought that I was simply playing 'the religion card' to get leniency. This saddened me, because although I could see their point of view and understand their cynicism, my life had genuinely changed.

Towards the end of the trial's second day they asked me if I wanted to testify. 'Yes,' I replied simply. But even as I said that word, which I had agreed with my barrister, I had this incredible sense that actually I should be saying the opposite. In the midst of the court hearing, I suddenly felt very confused. Surely God wasn't telling me to remain silent and not even take the opportunity of explaining myself?

I thought back to the verse which God had given me in my bedroom – Matthew 9:6, 'Son, your sins are forgiven; take up your bed and go home.' And I remembered what I'd felt God say to me, 'Dez, I have forgiven you of your sins. You're not going to prison, you're going home.'

Before, I had been excited by this, running around and telling everyone what God had said, but now I was unsure. Had I just been believing a lie, conjured up by my own imagination? The facts said that I was going to prison, yet I believed that God had told me different. That night, Sheila and I went back to my parents' new house in Essex, near my aunt's, and decided that the best thing to do was just pray. We must have been praying for thirty or forty minutes non-stop, when something happened that neither of us had ever experienced before. Very suddenly, I felt this presence come into the room. I opened my eyes and looked at Sheila – from her frightened appearance I could tell that she could feel it, too. That presence and the feeling are still impossible for me to explain – all I can say is that it was undoubtedly the presence of God, right there in the room with us. I felt like I couldn't speak; all I wanted to do was be reverent; to acknowledge that this presence was God. Finally I did manage to say something.

'The thing is over there isn't it?' I stuttered, pointing to one corner of the room.

'Yes,' she whispered back to me. 'How did you know?'

'I can feel it, too.'

Then we were both silent again. It was in the midst of that silence that God said something to me – like a silent voice that I couldn't hear but couldn't deny either.

'Don't speak in court,' he said. 'Don't say anything. I am your judge, I am your vindicator. Do not speak in court tomorrow.'

This was mad . . . but this was God. I made up my mind then – I would not speak in court the next day.

On the third day of the trial, when I had been due to speak, I did just what God had asked of me. The experience in my room gave me the boldness to tell the barrister that I wouldn't testify, which he'd already told me was a choice I had. The barrister looked a bit confused but shrugged his shoulders and simply said, 'Fine, it's your choice.' Having had my experience, part of me wanted to share with him how God had told me to say no.

In the courtroom, the judge asked me to get up to speak, but my barrister sheepishly explained my change of heart. Of course, part of me wanted to explain what had happened – just to put across a sense of sincerity and a sense that I was sorry that it had happened. I'd always thought that the best way of doing that would be from the witness box. But God had said no, and perhaps that was because he knew that if I had spoken, I'd have been torn to shreds in the cross-examination. After all, he is all-knowing . . .

Partly because of my silence, the trial seemed to speed up and it was clear that it wasn't going to last the full two weeks. We were only a little way through day three, and already the jury were being asked to make a decision. With all of this suddenly feeling so real, what I thought I knew seemed far too unreal to make sense. How could it be that I would not be going to prison for this charge? We weren't talking about a simple wounding here, but murder – the ending of someone's life at my hands. To weigh things even further against me, I'd discovered that the man I'd killed had been a soldier and that his father was a top policeman. And God was saying to me that I shouldn't even speak up to defend myself? I wasn't so sure that it made sense. During a break in proceedings, I went to the Old Bailey's toilets and prayed. As I did so, I felt that God spoke to me clearly, telling me to open my Bible and read the third chapter of Galatians. It wasn't a voice that I could hear, but more like my conscience quite clearly saying 'Galatians 3'.

I went into one of the cubicles, pulled the Bible out of my pocket and turned to the passage. In shortened terms it said:

You foolish Galatians! Who has bewitched you? . . . After beginning with the Spirit, are you now trying to attain your goal by human effort? . . . Does God give you his Spirit and work miracles among you because you observe the law, or because you believe what you heard?

It goes on to say that God is greater than the law. At that moment, I realised that although the law was going to judge me, I was there standing in faith. To me, those verses meant that God was going to be gracious – it was like God was saying to me, 'Don't be deceived by the law; don't fall into the hands of the law. Know that I am God and I am able to keep you and look after you.' I read it, and my fears were quietened; my confidence in God returned. And while that did not fully stop the raging battle in my mind, these verses did give me something to anchor on to.

They spent hours going over their decision, but couldn't arrive at one, so they came back out into the court, and it looked very likely that we'd have to wait at least another day for the verdict. They spoke to the judge for a little while, and then retired again. All this time I was wondering, would they come back and say 'guilty', or 'not guilty'? That one word could mean a whole world of difference to me. And nagging at the back of my mind was the thought that they might come back with the dreaded 'guilty, life conditional' verdict, which meant that I'd definitely be serving a life sentence. All this time, although I worried, I held firm to my faith. I was sitting there, now, having been charged with murder and waiting for the court to proceed and tell me how long I would be sent to prison for. God had told me, in terms so bizarre that I had to believe him, that he would get me through this somehow.

'Dez, I have forgiven you of your sins. You're not going to prison, you're going home.'

Finally, at the end of that third day, the jury foreman announced that they had arrived at a decision. As I heard him say this, my heart quickened to triple speed. This was it.

'Would the defendant please stand?' said the judge, as if we were in some kind of television drama. He turned to the foreman. 'Have you reached a verdict?'

'We have,' said the foreman, without blinking.

'Is it unanimous?'

'It is.'

The judge paused and looked across at me. Then he asked, 'On the charge of murder, do you find the defendant guilty, or not guilty?'

I wasn't looking at the judge so much, more just looking across into nothing and simply waiting. I think at that point, I was digging myself into what I now understand as faith.

'Not guilty.'

Had I heard that right? Not guilty? Seriously? My heart leapt as I processed those words – I almost even made the mistake of celebrating.

The judge interrupted my speeding train of thought. 'And on the charge of manslaughter, do you find the defendant guilty or not guilty?'

'Guilty.'

Every one of my internal organs seemed to drop through the floor. I began to stare at a little glass on the table in front of me, not really taking in the next words that the judge said. Guilty of manslaughter. I knew I was looking at about eight years. But at that moment, something inside me said, 'Dez, have faith – Galatians 3.'

The judge seemed to go on talking for an age but I couldn't really hear him. Later on, I got some of the court transcripts. Part of what the judge had said was that he felt strongly the need to respect and acknowledge the role of the jury. Because they had requested leniency, he felt the need to be mindful that they made this request after hearing all the evidence and all the information of the trial.

In the midst of all that, and just as I began to listen to him again, he explained that he did not see that a custodial sentence would be the right judgement. That, he believed, would just add more hardship to this young person and this family, and would set me off on the wrong road when I was showing signs of rehabilitation. As he explained this, I was surprised by some of the things which were taken into account. For instance, the fact that I gave the knife to my dad, even before knowing that my victim was dead, really went in my favour. To the judge and jury, that showed something positive about my character – and, perhaps, that I had not intended to kill. They believed from all the evidence put before them by people like my pastor, that I was someone who was willing to change his ways – who had turned the corner.

So thanks to the fact that I had no previous criminal record, that my character references were good, and that this incident seemed to be out of character to them – although that wasn't quite true – they'd decided to go easy. One thing I really did hear was this: 'Desmond Brown, I sentence you to two years probation.'

At which point my legs nearly went from beneath me, because all kinds of reality had hit me. I wasn't going to prison! God had kept his promise! In the gallery I heard my mum cry out. And then very quickly it seemed like we were on the move; on our way out, not to prison as, surely, every single person in there had fully expected, but home. As I left, I wanted to go and speak to the family of the deceased, to say that the person who'd taken their son's life was not the same person standing there – that this was a new person. But I had to understand that their world was now crumbling further even than it had already, and that this was not what they would be wanting to hear.

I walked out of there a free man, and even more importantly, knowing that God had impacted my world and my life in a quite incredible way. From that very moment, I had a real passion to serve him, fuelled by this incredible story and the absolute, unswerving knowledge that he both existed and took an interest in my life.

We celebrated modestly – it certainly wasn't a big party with 'Welcome Home Dez!' banners – just a glass of wine with some friends and family. Somehow, in the eyes of all these people who were not Christians and therefore didn't know God, a minor miracle had happened, and now they could celebrate. I was home, and the dark period of the last few months was finally drawing to a close.

All along, part of me had subconsciously accepted that I had committed this crime, and that I deserved to pay for it. In prison, before I was a Christian, I remember sitting there quite depressed, thinking that this couldn't go on for ever; that there had to come a day when it would finish, whether that was ten or fifteen years on. There had to come a time when they would say, 'Dez, it's over, you can go now.' It couldn't last for ever, and now, by the grace of God, I'd reached that conclusion.

Or at least, that's what I thought.

EIGHT

Coming out of court that final day was a little sur-real. Although I truly believed I'd be coming out, the fact that it was all over now just made me realise that my whole life was ahead of me. Sometimes in life there are things that loom so large on your hori-zon that you can't see past them; now this was over, I could suddenly begin to think about the future again.

I was aware that, by his grace, God had pulled me out of that situation, and it was towards him that my thoughts immediately turned on my release. I knew that there were certain areas of my life and behaviour which now had to be addressed – like sex before marriage. I had a lot of things to deal with. For instance, I continued to smoke drugs for about four months after becoming a Christian. I kept up sexual relations with my girlfriend, too. Even though we both had the intention to stop, it seemed that we'd keep falling into the same cycle of brief success and eventual failure as we tried to practise abstinence.

At the same time as trying to rebuild my spiritual life, I was also wrestling with pressing issues concerning where I would go from here. I began looking for work, and thinking about what sort of job I could get. To be honest, after all that I'd been through, I wasn't thinking about a career so much as a starting point in employment. Before my experience of God, I would have shied away from hard work and low-paid jobs; now, I was certain that this was what God wanted me to be doing.

I got a job in a local barber's shop which didn't pay well but gave me a springboard into the community and the world of work. I used that job, which gave me the opportunity to talk and engage with customers on a regular basis, to tell a lot of people about the changes and the events that had taken place in my life. I didn't do this directly – I wasn't hitting every customer over their newly-trimmed head with a Bible – but there were specific people who I grew naturally closer to, and out of those relationships sprang the opportunities to share in an unforced way. One of the people who I particularly talked to happened to be a friend of my brother who worked alongside me in the barber's. He wasn't a Christian but over time and various conversations I began to share my faith with him (this, I'd been told, was what Christians call evangelism).

I also started talking a lot about God with my mum. I think by that time she had realised that my faith was not just a passing phase but something that was obviously very significant and real to me. Mum had seen a definite change in my character, and that said more to her than any words could have done. She, herself, had no real experience of church and Christianity, and so had nothing to compare my experience to. There were a lot of pressing issues in her life at that time – she was in a heap of debt and felt like the whole family had been broken up. Her big problem with the Christianity I presented to her was this: if God was a God of love, then how come there are people around the world suffering? And if God really does care for us, then how come all this is happening to me? I could understand her questions – I wasn't sure that I was qualified to answer them.

We kept talking though – sometimes our conversations in the kitchen would turn so deep and emotional that we'd both be sobbing. And though I clearly didn't have all the answers, as I continued to share about the unshakeable fact that God does care, and truly loves us, my mum gradually came to a point at which she made a commitment to follow him.

It wasn't an instantaneous thing – it was over the three or four months following my release that my mum gradually moved towards that commitment. But eventually it did happen and, almost as soon as it did, her life and attitudes began to radically change.

My dad, who saw all this happen, had been a lay-preacher back in Jamaica. However, having arrived in this country and seen the hypocritical way in which Christians, or so-called Christians, had treated him, he had turned his back on the faith. So, because of his past and his awareness of what Christianity was supposedly all about, he was watching me from a safe distance to see, not so much what I was saying, but how I was living. He kept that watching distance for a while and didn't respond as quickly as my mum had. One day, though, it got to the point where he could no longer deny the massive impact that God had made in my life, and he, too, became a Christian.

To me, Christianity had provided me with the ultimate truth. It was the answer to why humans exist; why I was here. Before I'd encountered Christianity, my attitude was that you just live your life how you want to and make the most of it. Life was not about where I was going to be eternally, but simply about the here and now. Coming to Christianity raised a whole bunch of new questions. I realised that we are

eternal beings – this life is just a blink of an eye compared to the real picture – and the way we live here
and now will determine our future. I'd certainly
begun to talk well about living a different kind of
life, but I soon realised that talk is cheap. Unless you
actually live differently and deal with the areas of
your life in which you have been living the wrong
way then you are going to spend eternity separated
from God.

Within me a passion had welled up to tell people
about God. There was this joy in me, like someone
who'd learned a fantastic secret and desperately
needed to share it with their friends. Around me at
that time I'd seen a lot of other young people make
commitments to Jesus, and I'd seen how their lives
had changed. Coming from our street background
we still had struggles with issues like sex and drugs.
God was still the truth though; as I understood it the
problems and struggles were part of me, not part of
that truth. And with God living inside me, and my
faith growing, those things were becoming less and
less dominant in my mind and desires day by day.
Once God is inside of you, he slowly begins to alter
the way you think and the way you feel – that's just
the natural fruit of his power working in you.

I'd talk to all of my old friends about this good
news, this secret I had to share. I was so forceful at

times that they ended up getting a bit agitated by me. Although I was a rough diamond, God had made me this irrepressible vessel for his message. I'd even speak to friends of friends, or their parents, or their uncles! They, too, found my directness difficult, because I was so up-front and passionate. And yet, because I had my own story to back it up, which they knew had more than a ring of truth about it, they found it hard to argue with me. Despite my admitted struggles – nobody is made perfect overnight, after all – the thing that really seemed to impact them was the way in which I lived, and the radical change in lifestyle which I had so clearly implemented.

That became challenging though, and I didn't always pass the test. I had this one friend who sold drugs, and every time I went round to his place with the objective of sharing Jesus, I ended up smoking drugs with him. This was obviously not showing him that Christianity is a life-changing experience – but more of an add-on. Clearly, things couldn't continue like this, and it was an area in my life that God really had to deal with. I felt him speak to me – giving me the picture of the recovering alcoholic. That alcoholic, if he has any sense or good advice, doesn't go back into a pub, at least for a long while after he has made it through recovery. In the

same way, for me, it didn't make sense to be spending time with someone who took and sold drugs –
even if my motives were to share my faith with him
– when I was still addressing my own long-term
issues with drugs. For some people, a conversion to
Christianity brings a total overnight change in every
area of their life. But I was just being real in admit-
ting that, for me, this wasn't the case, and that some
areas still needed a lot of polishing.

When I was 18, I returned to college and finished off
my diploma in construction. They'd given me a few
papers while I was in prison, but I wasn't in there
long enough to finish it. The college was gracious,
though, and allowed me to return the following
year and finish a few modules so that I could complete the course and gain the qualification.

I saw college as my new mission field. I would
regularly share my faith there with anyone who'd
listen, and although I can't say that there were mass-
es of people who made a commitment to God, I do
know that people would listen because they knew
what I'd been like and where I'd come from.

My life had truly changed and, as a result, I could
look back on the offence that I had committed with
very different eyes. I was so sorry for what had happened, and felt an enormous swell of sympathy for

the family of my victim. But beyond that, I could now look back soberly and see the real reason why I had committed that crime: pride.

When I returned to college, my path crossed again with that of a guy who, prior to my spell in prison, had been my enemy. I'd always seen him as a plum, by which I mean that he was a small guy, with a lot of mouth, who could be silenced quickly enough if you gave him a slap. One day, when neither of us were in college, he brought up some friends from Tottenham, to confront me and let me know that if I didn't keep my head down, there were going to be problems between us. He just wanted to show me there were people behind him, and create a bit of fear and tension.

In the past, such a visit would have enraged me, irritating my sense of pride so much that I'd not have been able to stop myself from proving a point to him. But now I was a Christian, and a different Dez, so, the next time I saw him, waiting for a bus, I walked over and spoke to him softly.

'Look,' I said, 'I know how I carried on in the past, but I just want to say that I'm sorry if I have done anything against you. Let's just call it quits and let's have peace between us.'

I put my hand out to shake his and this guy sucked his teeth and looked me up and down.

Though I'd known it was the right thing to do, it was also incredibly hard and, at that moment, I wished the ground would swallow me up. He didn't shake my hand, but that wasn't important. In that moment, it became clear to me that God was influencing me in a dynamic way, continuing the process of changing me.

I had another experience of this a few weeks later after a big Christian meeting in Tottenham. While I was there I saw that a lot of people were being touched by the power of God, but to be honest that wasn't really my experience. I was hungry to feel God close at that time, and left feeling a little frustrated. However, I didn't realise that God was going to be heavily involved in my evening as I reached the bus stop. As I waited for the bus with my brother-in-law-to-be and two people from our church, I noticed this guy standing behind me. I saw him bouncing up and down with his hands in his pockets and straight away, being street-minded, I realised that this guy had something in his pocket. From the way that he was looking at me, still rocking and clutching something within his coat, I was sure he was going to pull out a weapon and hit me with it. Glancing at him again, I noticed that it was Nickergee who I'd had a fight with when I'd been in prison – the one who had sent me faeces. I spun around to face him and, as I did so, words came out of my mouth that just seemed appropriate for that time:

'Nickergee – I haven't seen you for ages!' I said, smiling as widely as I could through my obvious concern, 'You're from prison aren't you?'

Words continued to tumble out of my mouth, and I knew they weren't my own – I'd never have been able to be so diplomatic with a man who might be looking to cut or batter me with a tool.

'I know that we had problems when we were in prison,' I continued. 'But I've changed. I've become a born-again Christian!'

As I was talking, he was staring at me, as if to say: a) are you on this planet? And b) are you for real? Again, I put my hand out, along with the words, 'Sorry mate.' As I spoke, though, his bouncing became less pronounced, and his grip on whatever the object in his coat was, loosened.

I stood there, looking at him and squirming. It was another of those hideous 'I'd like to disappear' moments, where after thirty seconds my hand was still out there waiting. Eventually though, unlike my other old enemy, Nickergee placed his hand in mine, and shook it. Slowly, we started talking – about how my life had changed, and, like anyone who's come out of prison, about my case and his.

So there were two significant instances, just in the short time that I had been out on probation, that were genuinely about God dealing with my old problem, pride. I still carry those vivid memories with me today.

Shortly after these minor incidents happened, I was called back to the court for an appeal. I had quite an immature understanding of faith, and of God. Because he had spared me from prison in the original court case, I had taken it as read that God obviously didn't ever want me to go to prison. And because I now knew that God was for me and with me, I was sure that I couldn't now end up being sent to prison as a result of this appeal. I was in the same situation as last time, and so, perhaps naturally, because I'd come out last time, I began telling everybody not to worry and that I was certain that I was not going to prison. The more and more I was saying it, the more I managed to convince myself that it was the truth. However, the closer it got to the appeal trial, the more I began to question myself. This didn't feel the same as it did last time. Last time, I hadn't been trying to convince myself – rather there was a kind of knowing inside of me, that God's promise to keep me from prison was a fact. The night before going to the Court of Appeal, having been free in the outside world for over four months (this was June), I remember going into my mum's room and praying. When I prayed, the thing that hit my heart was that God had not been telling me that I'd get off this time – I had simply been try-ing to convince myself through a kind of strong will and strong thinking. Suddenly, I knew that there weren't any guarantees that I would avoid prison. Calmly, I managed to go downstairs and tell Sheila that I wasn't feeling sure anymore. I didn't want to worry her, though, and so remained reassuring. And the main reason that I didn't want to worry her was that something very significant had happened. Sheila was pregnant.

On that, more later, but right at that moment we had a judgement call to make. We had already agreed that soon we needed to tell both her parents and mine about the baby – but as yet she wasn't showing. Reluctantly, we decided to get the court hearing out of the way first and then tell them.

At the Court of Appeal, there was to be one hearing where three judges compared my original trial to other court cases of similar gravity. The case against me argued that it was wrong to give somebody two years probation for this offence when two or three years ago someone who had committed a similar offence got eight to ten years. The judges compared cases, and agreed that the original sentence had been too light.

So that was it. My punishment was being removed, and replaced with something which they felt to be more fitting. I was almost certainly going to prison.

On the one hand, this young person who had been attending his probation, was being rehabilitated, and who was now going to church. Although they looked at all these positives, there were two other factors which would influence their decision. The first angle was rehabilitation and, clearly, I did well on that. But the second one was justice, and the appeal against the original ruling claimed that justice had not yet been done. And while I was clearly not the same person who'd killed someone more than a year earlier, there was probably a feeling among them that the sentence handed out did not adequately punish the taking of a life. They must have believed that they needed to show at least some measure of discipline and take steps toward deterring other people from committing offences like this.

The whole process, of removing one sentence and replacing it with another, happened right there and then, in front of my eyes. Their decision was swift and biting.

'Desmond Brown, you are to serve a two-year custodial sentence.'

And then I literally had a couple of minutes to say my goodbyes. Probation had ended, and a real sentence had begun. Having been a free man when I entered the court, I was now going to be led away in handcuffs. It was a hugely emotional moment – Sheila was crying uncontrollably, as were other friends and family. Strangely though, I wasn't. I was just focussed on doing what I needed to do next. I gave my belongings, money and keys over to my mum, said my hasty goodbyes, and then complied totally as they led me down to the cells.

Back into prison, then, and this time, for the long haul.

NINE

The people down in the court cells must have thought I was crazy, because as soon as I went down there, I started preaching about Jesus. For instance, right away I saw two guys – I can't remember what they were in there for. I told them what had just happened to me, the whole testimony. I've just been sentenced to a two-year imprisonment and I'm finding random people to tell them how Jesus Christ has changed my life.

Before they take you away to prison, you're allowed one visit, so I got to see my girlfriend. Sheila had just been spending time with my probation officer, explaining to her that she was pregnant and that nobody in our families knew. The probation officer offered her support in telling the family but, even still, it must have been very distressing for Sheila to have to go home after this. She tried to be brave when we met, but I could see how upset and afraid she was. As we sat there together, it was with a sense of disbelief that we ran through the events of the last few months together: the incident, my month in custody, the changes that had happened in my life. Now, more recently, we'd discovered that she was pregnant and suddenly I'd been given two years imprisonment. We hugged and tried to be strong for each other.

Before the appeal, I'd begun to believe that going inside couldn't have been God's will, but I think afterwards I had begun to understand a little more about God. At the time of my first trial, the time was wrong for me to be in prison, but now things had changed and the time was right. No one can know the mind of God, but perhaps he kept me out of prison for those four months – quite miraculously I guess – so that he could accomplish many things in my life. There was nothing in me that felt let down by God, and certainly nothing that believed this sentence necessary, in some way, for me to be truly repentant or forgiven. But it was where God, the most important being in the universe, wanted me to be now. The fact that I accepted this so readily, perhaps showed a little glimpse of how far God had brought my character. Where previously I had been dominated by pride, now there was a sense of humility.

On another level, my conscience had always held to the idea that if you do the crime, you do the time. So I didn't see this as being unjust anyway. Two years was nothing for that offence, and I would not have seen it as unjust if I'd been served a much harsher sentence. That said, when you get given two years, those two years look like twenty in your mind, especially if you haven't been to prison for that long before. You can't think beyond it – those seven hundred-plus days just seem like an unconquerable wall of time.

However, my feeling at that time was more and more that God was in control. So now these two years would be dedicated to serving him, and would be a sacrifice to him. When people asked me, then, if I was OK about my revised sentence, I would answer, 'Yes', but not because it would prove that I'd 'done my time'. Instead, I thought, '*If this is the way God wants it, then this is what must happen.*'

My issues with drugs had eased in the previous couple of months. I had drifted away from a lot of my friends who used to smoke drugs, and I'd moved to a new area where I didn't really have any drug-smoking friends. The 'link' that I had been getting drugs from initially had been weakening, and I also had this overwhelming conviction that it was wrong. I couldn't be going around saying that I was a Christian and not addressing this. For my problems with drugs and sex outside of marriage (which the Bible says hurts God), my prayer was simple enough: 'God help me, God help me. Give me the strength and let me understand.'

In the case of the drugs, it meant stopping going to the house of the person who was my 'link'. Then, because the drugs I was involved in were more of a psychological addiction than chemical or physical, it was a matter of committing myself to God and being focussed on what it was that he now wanted me to live for.

My big issue with sex outside of marriage was understanding what was wrong with it. To me, it was a pleasurable thing, a good thing, a legal thing, a healthy thing and part of the culture I was used to. Sheila and I truly loved each other, and I couldn't honestly understand what could be wrong with an expression of love. If at first I'd simply said a blanket 'no' to sex outside of marriage without understanding why, then that would have simply been unthinking and legalistic. I don't believe Christianity is about doing what the Bible says without thinking. I think it's about using your mind, engaging with the reasons why God asks certain things of us. Then you use your will to make a choice and own the responsibility for that choice.

Slowly, Sheila and I did begin to understand the reasons – God made sex as a special gift for within marriage, in order to help protect and prosper it. Also, being sexually active was not an upright representation of the lifestyle that God has called single Christians to live, so we knew that people might label us hypocrites or irrelevant if we continued in our old ways. Understanding these things really helped to lead us to an informed decision about the issue.

Having only been a Christian for a few months, people hadn't been jumping in my face with questions like, 'Are you guys sleeping together?' and, 'Are you guys on drugs?' People weren't screaming at us, telling us what we shouldn't be doing. We were fortunate not to find ourselves in a judgemental church. Instead, people would simply say, 'How's everything going? How's your family? We're praying for you.' At that time, in the early stages, they were much more concerned about welcoming us into the church and the faith with open arms. The challenges, they felt, could wait a little longer.

I started my sentence in Brixton prison, where I was allocated to G-wing. Last time, I'd found myself on F-wing which, as I explained, was one of the two most notorious wings in the prison. G-wing wasn't a particularly bad wing – more of an allocation wing. Two long years stood between me and a reunion with Sheila and my parents, or at least, that's how I saw it, not understanding of course that after as little as eight months I could be out on probation.

Things seemed to have moved on in the prison. Although I had to share a cell with someone else, they had started putting in toilets and sinks, so I no longer had to put up with the old slop-out system. My cell mate was younger than me by about a year – a guy from Stonebridge who'd been jailed for various drugs offences, including smoking crack. Obviously he wasn't allowed drugs in prison, so he was going through cold turkey. Having a lot of experience of drugs myself, I knew only too well how uncomfortable he must have been. He'd been used to having certain chemicals in his body and suddenly the supply of those chemicals had been ripped away. He was getting cold sweats, feeling paranoid, getting agitated. Although he'd been in there a while before I came in, I was able to offer him some comfort and stability. I was only in there with him for about a week, but during that week I was able to share my faith with him. And although you might imagine this would be the last thing he'd want to hear about, I can honestly say that he was very interested. When you're in a cell with someone for hours and hours on end, it gives you great opportunities to get to know them a bit. And once you get to know them, they want to know about you, so it becomes a very natural place to share about faith.

By the time I'd moved out, he had not made any formal commitment to following Jesus. He'd heard me praying and had even prayed a little himself. Perhaps our brief friendship sowed a seed which God watered in another way later on in his life. Perhaps God is still wanting to do that. I didn't know – but, as I saw it, I didn't need to know; I just needed to plant a seed and leave the rest to God.

During that week I had a lot of time to sit and reflect on my new situation. Through conversations with other prisoners, it became clear to me that 'two years custodial' rarely meant 730 days inside a prison cell. I began thinking, 'OK, how long have I got?' What did 'two years' actually mean? Did it mean two years, sixteen months or even less? At this early point, I was still struggling to understand the system, because there are all these 'dates' to think about: parole, EDR and LDR. Parole is when they consider you for parole, EDR is your earliest possible date of release and LDR is latest date of release. That meant that my two-year sentence was broken down into three stages: eight months, sixteen months and the full two years. At any time between eight and sixteen months I could get parole, (eight months was the earliest I could possibly get parole) but there was absolutely no guarantee that I ever would. It was just about conceivable that in a best-case scenario, I could possibly get parole on my EDR. But with a crime like mine, which was so serious, with what was still quite a light sentence attached, I wondered if they would even consider me for parole. All this was spinning through my head on a daily basis. I tried to suppress the constant desire to work out exactly what 'two years' meant, but it was only human nature that it continued.

I was sitting in my cell one night towards the end of that first week, when somebody called out the name 'Aubrey'. That was a fairly striking and unusual name, and I remembered it from somewhere – it connected in my mind to this guy I'd had a fight with in prison. Then I remembered: it was his friend. Everyone began calling his name and giving him respect. It is a common thing in prison to shout out through the windows; so you can be in your cell and hear three or four different conversations going on. They'll talk about various things: sometimes people are just shouting at someone for favours, others are just cussing, and still others are having genuine chats.

Anyway, on this evening, it seemed like everyone on the wing was calling out this guy's name, and all of them were giving him respect. I could tell by the tone and the language going on that this respect was genuine. Straight away, my thought was that this guy was a plum. I knew Aubrey, and he wasn't by any means hard. So, my train of thought careered, if he's got respect, and I know he's a plum, then if he gets a good slap from me, I'll get all the respect.

So that old nature of mine, which I'd foolishly believed was now dead and buried, started to kick in again. All these feelings and emotions began to kick in. He didn't know I was in there, but I knew he was there. I could also see that people were giving him respect, while I knew that he was a plum. So my whole nature was now thinking that I should get him in order to raise myself up above him in the prison pecking order. The whole culture of prison was beginning to impact my thoughts and senses, and if my thoughts could have been put on paper at that moment, you would not have guessed that I was a Christian. Yet, at the very same time, I was also thinking, *'No, God, I still want to be a Christian while I'm in here – God I still want to serve you, you've been faithful to me.'* So there was a war going on with an angel and a devil on each of my shoulders.

That night, I lay there thinking and praying hard. I really asked God for help, and the next day, when I saw Aubrey, I felt differently. Rather than fight with him, we talked openly and honestly – I told him that I'd become a Christian, of course, but we also spoke about the beef that I'd had with his friends, and also about the stabbing in which I was injured. Now I knew that what I was saying would mean that I was perceived as having come off worse in the fight, and that hit my pride. But God was dealing very directly with my pride – the issue which I had once found so overwhelming. I knew Aubrey was thinking, '*So – you're not as hard as you thought you were*' and, as a result, I would never have the opportunity to argue the point. But now I was a Christian – and Christians do not fight. At this time, all sorts of positive and negative thoughts were kicking off inside my head, but I held my cool. In the very best kind of way, God really humbled me through this situation.

There was more divine intervention a few days later as, again, God proved that he was with me through my struggles and that he was far bigger than any of them. Usually when you get moved out of one prison and into another, you get told the night before. That's to prepare you for the fact that you've got to get up at 6 a.m. the next morning, have an early breakfast, get your belongings and go. But that's not what happened when they moved me. Just at that time, my cell mate had taken in some drugs (he had swallowed a bag containing drugs – a very risky smuggling technique), and was due to pass them through his system. In my head, a battle was being fought as another dilemma was posed. Could I smoke them with him? Obviously, we were in a cell together, so he was bound to offer me the chance to share them. This challenged me – drugs being one of my last big unreconciled issues, and in my heart, I had this feeling that I was going to cave in and compromise. I knew it was wrong, and yet I began to justify in my own mind that it wasn't *that* wrong. But, thankfully, it never came to that. The next morning, just before my cell mate was due to pass the drugs through his system, there was an unexpected banging at the door. Although I wasn't due to be moved from Brixton, the voice at the door clearly said, 'Brown, you're being shipped out.'

God knew that if I had relapsed then, my whole prison sentence might have panned out very differently, so he stepped in, I got moved, and within minutes I was on my way back to Feltham.

I had my own room in Feltham, where many people thought I was slightly mad. This was because I used to worship God in my cell – singing loudly with my hands lifted up above my head. If anyone came along and looked in, they would have either seen me like this or praying. God had moved me out of a situation that was beyond me; he knew how much I could take, and so his intervention was a catalyst for me to give him praise.

I was barely in Feltham long enough to catch my breath. After my week of prayer and praise – having done little to allay the rumour that I was a madman – the decision was taken to move me to Warren Hill, in Ipswich. The other convicts, some of whom seemed to know the ins and outs of every prison in the land, told me that it was an OK prison but more like an old DC (detention centre). It was a don't-walk-on-the-grass, make-up-your-bed, clean-your-cell kind of place, which operated with some of the old DC traits. The warders would still come in and do a room check, for instance, so I'd feel somewhere between a modern prisoner and a prisoner of war.

I moved there after barely a week in Feltham, into what I discovered was predominantly a white man's prison. It was also a prison into which they put problematic people or those who potentially could be. All in all, it didn't sound too great. It was a category C institution – a closed prison, and so quite strict.

In reality, as most of the people in there came from the country, it wasn't a real challenge or full of problems. However, when you've got ten or twenty extreme cases in there, there's always the potential for trouble. So it was very different to Feltham, where everybody was chaotic and from London – this was more of a rural prison with the odd nutcase thrown in to spice it all up.

There was no black and white confrontation, so I felt chilled. Also, I thought it would be less challenging. I'd always wanted to do my prison sentence in an adult prison like this, because young offenders' institutes are – according to those around the prison circuit – just too hyper. When you go in to young offenders' prison, generally it's very lively, with plenty of fights and little respect for one another. When you go into an adult prison, the other prisoners are usually much more mature. They just want to get on with their time and get out. If something kicks off, then it kicks off, but it doesn't usually happen for something silly – it would have to be something serious. In a young offenders' prison though, someone would come in for two weeks and want to get themselves a name and gain a little notoriety, so they'd end up chucking hot tea over someone else. They are a bit more naïve and get too excited.

I hadn't been too keen on staying in Feltham then, as it was just a bit too lively, especially for a Christian who wanted to keep his head down and just do his time. So when I went to Warren Hill, a calmer, rural prison, it was cool, and I made friends among like-minded people quite quickly. Just as before, I began sharing my faith with my new friends. Some people did not like that, including the officers – in fact more so the officers.

I found out after being in there a little while that Elton was in Dover prison. My parents were having to do a lot of travelling, visiting me in Ipswich and him in Dover, so they put in a request that one of us be moved so that we were both in the same prison. This request was approved, and so they moved Elton to Ipswich.

However, while he had been in Dover, he'd been banged up next to Isaiah-Raymond Dyer, a former enemy of mine who had since become a Christian (Isaiah-Raymond is now the lead singer with the internationally successful gospel group, 'Raymond & Co'). Isaiah-Raymond had become a Christian while he was in Dover and was in a cell right next door to my brother's. So he began to tell Elton about God, and the change he'd made in his life and, before long, Elton became a Christian. It wasn't the first time my brother had heard about the gospel, because Sheila's brother and I had both been sharing with him before he went into prison. So these were seeds that were sown over time into Elton's mind, watered by God and eventually harvested by Isaiah-Raymond.

Just before my brother moved to my prison, he, too, had become passionate for God. He really wanted God to be near him all the time – in many ways I think it was his security in all that was going on. Although we were in different wings, we still saw each other regularly in the recreational time and we'd also go to chapel together. And while it was far from good that my brother was in prison at all, it was great to have my family in there with me, especially as Elton was not only my blood brother, but also now my brother in Christ.

I'd done about two months by the time Elton came in. While I was there, I got a job (I chose this above education), working on some scaffolding, painting the slim prison windows. The first day on the job, I went up on the scaffolding and got chatting to this guy who I didn't know. He was a tall man with long, flowing hair and piercing blue eyes. Halfway through the conversation I said to him, 'I'm a Christian. I believe in Jesus Christ, the Son of God.'

'Ah yes,' he replied. 'I'm Jesus.'

Now this was of some concern to me. I was standing on a scaffold, with a large man who was telling me that he was Jesus. Suddenly I was intensely aware of how high up I was, and how high on drugs he might be.

'Er, what are you talking about?' I asked gently.

'I'm Jesus,' he said again. 'That's my name.'

I was worried that I was up there with a lunatic.

'I mean,' he explained, 'that's my nickname, because of the way I look, and the hair.'

This was a moment of some relief, but somehow the tension didn't shatter. Jesus didn't seem to like me, partly because I was a Christian and partly because of the incident that had brought me into prison.

'How can you say that God loves you?' he asked aggressively. 'How can you say that I need forgiveness from God, and that he's forgiven you? Look what you've done – I'm not in here for killing someone! Who are you to preach to me?'

Interestingly, two or three years earlier I'd been involved in a big fight down in Romford where me and my friend beat up three guys, one of whom was Jesus' cousin. I'd heard about this guy because he was quite well known in Romford – not for looking like Jesus, but just because he could chuck it in a fight.

So this guy, Jesus, who I'm now working with up on a scaffold, is the cousin of one of the guys we battered. I saw this as God's humour, although of course I knew there was a chance that it might now kick off between us. So when we talked, we inevitably ended up getting round to the subject of this fight. It was yet another reason why he didn't like me. He began to get very agitated, partly because he didn't buy my whole 'finding God' story. He was pretty sure he had me figured out – that I was one of those many people in prison who say that they believe in God, but don't preach the gospel. They go to chapel, but their 'believing in God' means that they'll probably still have a bit of puff, still swear and still fight if they need to.

'Look,' I tried to explain, 'I know what you think of me. But I'm different. I don't smoke or swear and I'm not looking to fight – I just believe in Jesus and my life has genuinely changed.'

I'd love to say that at that point he fell onto his knees and repented, but sadly he didn't. In fact, he got so angry that he threatened to throw me off the scaffold. But who knows, perhaps, just as with my brother, I was simply sowing the seeds, and at some point in the future, someone else will harvest and Jesus will come to know Jesus.

Having been a rude boy on the street, but now maturing as a Christian, enabled me to kind of navigate my way through prison, being relevant to the prisoners, but not compromising. There were moments of relapse, but I never compromised to the point where it defaced my Christianity. Instead, people who'd got to know me for a while, and had been waiting for me to slip up, began to say, 'This guy's a real Christian'. I was praying for people constantly, and listening to tapes of preaching so much that other prisoners started to ask to borrow them. I had worship CDs in my cell, I didn't swear, I didn't take other people's food, I'd have a laugh, but it wouldn't get to the point where it was hurting somebody else.

Once people had begun to take me and my faith seriously, I became a sort of counsellor to the other inmates. People could see that I was streetwise and tuned in, and also that I was a Christian with sensible things to say. So if there was something going on or something kicking off, prisoners would think, 'Let's have a chat to Dez,' and ask me what I thought. Also, because I had gained a lot of respect in the prison, they would ask me if I wanted to get involved in something dodgy, and I would always say, 'No thanks, I don't see it as a good thing.' This had two effects – first, some bad things that might have happened did not, as people took my advice, and second, I got the nickname 'Preacher Brown'. It stuck, and that's what they began to call me. As I was walking round the prison they would shout out, 'Preacher'. Many people, though they respected me, were looking hard to see if I slipped up and proved their suspicions about 'Christians' right. They had possibly never seen someone inside genuinely living life as a Christian, and so, as they realised more and more that this truly was me and not some kind of mask, they began to ask, 'Should he even be in here?'

After a while, I became involved in the chapel services. I was involved with the small groups which ran there, too, because my knowledge of God and the Bible was quite advanced considering I was in prison. I could answer a lot of questions, and that further enhanced my reputation as 'Preacher Brown'.

Six months into my sentence, the time came to assess whether I was suitable for being moved to an open prison. At about the same time, I had to undergo another assessment to decide my parole date.

After an interview, they decided that they would move me to the open prison. This meant moving from a place where I spent my nights in a locked cell (and a lot of my days, too), to a place where there is no lock on the door and, if I wanted to, I could just walk out and run off. There is a lot more freedom in an open prison: you go to work and you get paid for doing carpentry. There are so many perks compared to say, a cat-C prison. There aren't even any bars on the windows.

At this point, surely 'Preacher Brown' should have been excited about the new possibilities for sharing the gospel of Jesus. But somehow, that wasn't what I felt. Instead, from nowhere, my old nature kicked in, and I had a relapse of my old ways. There was this guy on my wing in Warren Hill who I'd heard had got some drugs through. So, knowing that I was on the move, I shouted down to him to send me some stuff. He sent me up this cannabis and, for the first time in ages, I sat on my bed smoking it. I didn't get the kind of heavy buzz that I'd normally get from this, even though I hadn't been smoking for nearly a year. And yet, I remember at the same time sitting on my bed praying, 'God, help me. What am I doing?'

They moved me to the open prison the very next day. But instead of leaving the drugs behind and drawing a line under the incident, I took them in with me, because I knew that drugs are currency inside. Of course, to move and take drugs with you is a ridiculously silly thing to do, because you're very likely to get searched on arrival. Somehow though, I managed to escape that – discovery would certainly have extended my time inside – and I got the drugs in with me.

It quickly got worse. I made friends, almost instantly, with this guy who was in there for dealing drugs, and who clearly wasn't rehabilitating. He had an ounce of cannabis in his cell and he had a lot of respect for me because I knew my drugs and, more importantly, because I was from higher up in the pecking order, having been convicted of a serious crime. Here is a big, tall, black guy, he thought, who knows quite a lot of people, and who seems quite influential.

'Mate,' he said, 'if you look after my drugs in your cell, you can smoke whatever you want, and I'll sell the rest.'

At any other time in my sentence, I would have slammed this idea as quickly as it had arisen. But I didn't. I took him up on his offer, and practically abused it. For about a week, I hit a spiritual rock bottom. But in the midst of this, I was still praying – my belief and faith in God had not changed one iota – and I had a strange dream. In this dream, a Christian friend of mine, was standing next to me. He began to sing to God, and as he sang he started to ascend heavenwards. But I was still just standing there until, slowly, I began to disappear, bit by bit. My friend shouted down to me, 'Dez, quick – praise God, praise God!' So I joined him in singing, and as I sang my body began to reappear, and as I continued, I, too, joined him in ascending.

I woke up suddenly, sweating. *'Dez,'* I thought, *'spiritually you are dying and disappearing.'* I had to worship God again and quick – not only through singing, but also through my lifestyle.

The next evening, I prayed, 'God take this away from me – God take this away from me.'

I sat on my bed, torn between wanting to do what God wanted and my own insatiable desire for that artificial high. I was just about to build my spliff, and yet was still praying, 'God take this away from me.'

I could hear that the coast was clear and that there were no officers around.

'God take this away from me.'

Somebody across the landing, waiting for my 'seconds', called out for me to hurry up.

'God take this away from me.'

And then, God literally gave me the strength, and suddenly the craving had gone and I just didn't want it anymore. I got up, walked across the landing and knocked on this guy's door.

'That's it,' I said, as much to myself as to him. 'Forget it, no more drugs.' It broke his heart of course – he wasn't thinking about God, he was just thinking about his spliff.

The following day I got the stuff out of my cell and back into the hands of the dealer, who was disappointed but understood. Then I shared what had happened with an older Christian who used to come and visit me. He just prayed for me, encouraging me that this blip was over and that I was strong enough to get back into the lifestyle that God wanted for me. So for that week I had a spiritual relapse, but then, bam, I was back living passionately for God.

As my relapse came to an end, help to prevent me from doing the same thing again arrived in the shape of my brother, who was also moved to the open prison and ended up in the room two doors down from mine. So now we could go to one another's room, we could share our canteen, we could talk and encourage each other. Spiritually, this was a shot in the arm for me – now I had not only a brother but a fired-up Christian just a couple of doors along from me. We could pray together, and we even did 'fasts' together where we wouldn't eat food for three days, and only drink water. Together, praying, worshipping, evangelising and fasting, we became quite a dynamic force, and before long people began to be saved. One guy became a Christian within just a couple of days of Elton's arrival.

I think this really challenged the officers. One of them kept calling me a murderer, and although that may have been what he thought of me, I knew also that he and others were just digging at me because they could see that I was beginning to gain influence and that my evangelism was affecting other people's lives. I was doing this because of my faith, my belief, and yet they couldn't understand how I could say that God had forgiven me and was on my side, when I had killed someone. The fact that I was in prison meant I was guilty, and meant, to them, that I was a hypocrite. In most people's eyes there is little worse than taking someone's life, apart, perhaps, from rape and offences against children. So for them, I came in the worst kind of category, and yet I was telling them that God loved me, and that they needed to repent of all their sins. This one officer was so offended that I, of all people, was trying to tell him about God. Of course, having moved to a new prison, I had lost all the respect and credibility I'd built up in Ipswich. I had to start again and rebuild all that, so that people could see that what I was saying about the change in my life was really true.

I used to share my faith as I did my work, which was a kind of apprenticeship in carpentry. The man who was training me, and a number of others, was very upright, very stiff, a 'proper Englishman', who had been working in the prison service for years. He was interested in talking about God – he often used to think about matters of faith and was keen to talk about it. But he was an external tutor, which meant that I couldn't talk to him one to one. So instead, at times, the whole carpentry session would stop, for between half an hour and an hour, and everybody gathered around me, including him, asking me questions about God. Many of these questions searched beyond my growing understanding, and yet every time, God's wisdom seemed to come into my head and provide me with an answer. Somehow, although many of these people were more intellectual than me and had very sophisticated questions, everything got answered.

Meanwhile, on the outside, Sheila was about to have our baby. I knew that now I was in an open prison, I was likely to get compassionate leave if I asked for it, so with some confidence, I made my application. To my dismay, they declined my request. Now, I do not want to give the impression that in my relationship with God I was like a brainless slave. For a few days, the news that my request had been turned down even after I'd prayed hard about it really hit me – I wondered how it could possibly be that God was going to let me miss the birth of my own child. Instead of being there to hold Sheila's hand, I just received a phone call, telling me that she'd had the baby and that my new son was 8lbs 5oz. I spent that night crying in my cell, asking God why I couldn't have been there.

I did get to meet my son, Jordan, about a month later. My family came on a day visit to see both me and Elton, and obviously Sheila brought Jordan along with her. Seeing my boy for the first time was one of the most incredible moments of my life – I cried openly. I'd had photos, of course, but meeting him in the flesh was completely different. For the first time it truly struck me that this was my son. They gave me a whole day's release, too, which meant that I could leave the prison and spend the entire day with Mum, Dad, Sheila and the baby. It was a real high, but when they left, it was hard to take. I needed to be with them, Sheila and Jordan especially.

The interview for my parole arrived, where I had to see the assessment board for them to make a decision on a parole date. The way parole works is this: if for, instance, your date of release for parole (set at the beginning of your term) was the 1 May, then the board are allowed to make a decision on any date that is not earlier than that. But it could be any date from there until Christmas. I asked myself, considering the severity of my crime, whether it was possible that I'd get parole any time soon. Again, I felt that God spoke to me and told me that I was going to get parole. I didn't really think through what my response might be if I didn't get it, especially after missing the birth of my son.

Then, at my interview, my carpentry teacher asked me an unusual and searching question. 'Mr Brown, if you don't get parole, are you still going to believe in God?'

I wanted to be honest with them. My head was swimming with different thoughts, and I felt I knew this time that God had promised me parole. If that now didn't happen, where would that leave me? So I simply said, 'I don't know.'

Which was a huge thing to say, but I suddenly felt this need – swelled by the fact that my son was presently growing up without a dad – to get out. I couldn't have said that it was because I'd done my time, because I hadn't done much time at all, but whereas I'd been happy to remain inside up until now, suddenly it felt like completely the wrong place to be, and I needed to get out.

On Christmas Eve 1992, an officer came to me with a fax and said, 'Brown, you're out on 4 January.'

Talk about a Christmas present . . .

The parole board don't meet on 24 December, so to me this was just another miracle from God's own hand. I'll never know whether the message got delayed in the system, but that fax should not have arrived then. I was the only person in the whole prison who had been given their parole news on that day. How did this happen, how could this happen, I wondered? Even the officers commented on how unusual it was to get a fax through on Christmas Eve to say that someone had been given parole. Legally, 4 January 1993 was the earliest possible date on which I could have walked free, and that was the date I'd been given. I could have been kept in there until my EDR, which would have been August, or until my LDR which would have been April 1994 – and would have meant I'd served the whole two years. I had never really expected to leave the prison before August 1993, and yet now I was only ten days from freedom. Once again, God had proved himself to me, and in a way beyond anything that I could have expected.

On Christmas Day 1992, everybody on the wing apart from two people went to chapel, and by that time many, many people had made commitments to Jesus. The inmates still struggled and got into trouble, but they wanted to believe in Jesus, and they were committed to trying to change for him. As I came to leave, people were having Bible studies in the canteen, and while association was going on, there would be maybe six or eight people talking about God at any one time. It was like some sort of miniature revival, and yet God had brought all this from my brother and I coming to the prison.

TEN

After eight months inside, I got picked up on 4 January 1993, the only day that winter that it snowed. I collected my belongings, was given a small amount of money, and then released. Before I even reached the car outside the gates I could see that everyone was there – my baby, my parents, my girlfriend. And somewhere between that moment and my arrival back at home I realised that this really was it now. They couldn't send me back in there; no man had a claim over my life any longer. And I was certain that I would never do anything that would put me back in there.

I had been away from my beautiful girlfriend for a very long time. The church had told us that the rule was simple: Christians shouldn't have sex before marriage. But we'd barely shared a kiss in eight months – and we had a son together. Although our best intention was to stick to a no-sex rule, it just didn't happen. We fell back into the old cycle of sporadically falling sexually, then praying to God for strength and forgiveness, then falling again, and so on. We didn't ever decide that we may as well just sleep together – it was much more of an ongoing struggle and, perhaps, the last true tie to my old nature, now that God had finally slain my drug habit. I wanted to be with my son and I wanted to be with Sheila, so for a few days we stayed together. And, of course, because we had a son, this made it something of a grey area even for the church, although, ultimately, they and we agreed that it wasn't right. We didn't really want to make ourselves accountable to the church on this issue though, because that meant that we were going to be questioned on it.

A short while after my release, I started sharing a flat with a friend in Leytonstone. The flat was empty; there was literally nothing there apart from heating and a kettle. There was no flooring, no bedding, nothing, and so I had to get some stuff together in order to move in. Sometimes the heating ran out, as I didn't have much money, and it truly felt like I was starting from nothing. On the positive side, that helped to symbolise a true 'new start' in my life. On the negative side – I was broke!

In what was a slightly risky decision, I had moved in with a guy who was heavily into drugs. He would disappear for three or four days at a time, then he'd come back early one morning and just slump down somewhere in the flat. So although I wasn't taking them, drugs were around me again. And then something really unexpected happened. Sheila got pregnant again.

The first time it had happened, we'd been young and naïve. This time, we'd done it with the full Christian understanding of what is right and wrong. We knew that going against God's will is sin, and we worried, therefore, that since God doesn't want people to be pregnant outside of marriage, he didn't want the baby. And yet on the other hand, we knew that God is the giver of life, and that he loves every living thing. So we were really confused, obviously not wanting to tell anybody about what had happened, especially while Sheila wasn't show-ing. We were scared about what people would think of us – these Christians with two children outside of wedlock, with no jobs to speak of. Sheila came from an estate and from a single parent family. I had a significant criminal record. We knew that people would think we had no common sense, no wisdom, no maturity, no sense of responsibility. So because of all of that, we felt that we couldn't tell anyone. Yet in the midst of all these feelings, where Sheila and I were so desperate that we were actually asking God to take the baby away, I received an incredible phone call. It was my pastor:

'Dez,' she said. 'Sheila's pregnant isn't she?'

God had told her. It wasn't because she had seen Sheila, or that either of us had told her. It was just that God had told her, and she had not wasted any time in calling us, doing so without condemnation and with incredible grace. I have nothing but admiration for the way in which she pastored us – and not just the two of us, but our wider group. Me, Sheila and our friends were not the easiest people to pastor: armed robbers, drug addicts, homeless people – all of whom had become Christians, but who were very rough around the edges, and brought loads of baggage into the church. Most pastors have to cope with one or two of these kinds of people, but in us she had not one, not two, but fifteen or more young people who were just a rabble.

God gave her the right heart. She didn't just condemn us, but she challenged us, and it was exactly the same in this case. Her approach was that this needed to be dealt with, maturely and in the right way. So that's what transpired – we had to tell our parents, who took the news well, and then we had to stand up in front of the church and tell them that I had slipped up. Now, that might sound like a terrible thing, but I really owned it, thought carefully about what I was going to say and, with God's help, used it as a line in the sand.

'Look,' I said with all the honesty and genuineness in my heart. 'I've done wrong, I'm sorry. My life is a mess but I still love God, and if I've discredited you guys or the church in any way, please forgive me.'

That public apology brought true restoration between me, Sheila and our church, and the power of God fell on that meeting. People were sobbing as God touched their hearts, as he used our repentance and humility to impact all these other young people from all these other different situations. Sheila and I were sobbing too, and that was a great release for us as we didn't have to hide anything any more. Afterwards, many people came up to us and told us not to worry, encouraging us that while they didn't condone what we'd done, they still loved us and believed firmly that God loved us, too.

Sheila and I never slipped up sexually again. When our second child, Chanelle, was born, and subsequently Sheila and I married on 26 February 1994, there was a true sense of restoration, and of things being put right. On paper, Sheila and I looked like classic urban statistics – with children who were certain to follow our shabby leads – and yet, out of that, God formed something amazing: a happy home, and people full of love for one another, and for him.

I looked for a job for ages. Although I had basic construction qualifications, I really wanted to work with people. My whole view on life and on people had completely changed, and I now felt like more of a carer. I felt set free from my past – the mentality and attitude that had been so negative – and now I wanted to do a job that involved giving to and working with people. The big obstacle there, however, was my criminal record – anyone who goes for a job in the caring profession is going to be faced with police checks before long. As my offence was so recent, I was turned down, as police checks do not allow for character references and divine life changes.

Instead, I decided to bide my time and prove myself in another line of work. I got a job, late on in 1993, in a clock factory. Initially, the only work they could offer an ex-con with little in the way of qualifications was a cleaning job, where I would sweep the floor of the factory and clean the toilets. I was on the lowest rung of the ladder, but while in the past I would have seen this kind of work as beneath me, I now saw it as a chance to worship God. He had given me a second chance – a beautiful family, a release from prison and the backing of a good church. Doing this menial job to the very best of my ability would be a way of thanking him. The Bible explains worship as being a physical act – far beyond what we say or sing – and this job was my act of worship. Many people were shocked by the diligence and dedication which I, clearly an intelligent man, applied to floor sweeping.

The factory bosses took note, too, promoting me to the heady heights of the man who made the boxes to put the clocks in. Again, I did this job joyfully, thankfully, as an act of worship to my real boss. Over time, I was promoted again and again, until I found myself on the assembly line itself, helping to build the clocks. And while those promotions were a bonus, and certainly brought in more money, they were in no way connected to my dedication. Instead, perhaps, they were God's way of encouraging me, pushing me forward, and preparing me for the next stage in my life.

The next few years saw God really start to prosper me. It was as if he somehow responded to my worship to him, in taking on that job as a cleaner, and brought me on. Thankfully, it seemed that cleaning and clock assembly weren't the extent of his plans for me. In a sense, the years that came after that period of struggle and difficulty could make a book in themselves, but here I'll keep it brief.

While I climbed the ladder at the factory, and earned a basic wage at the same time, my heart was still very much set on a career in caring. I applied for help in this to an organisation called PATH (Positive Action Training in Housing), which specialised in working with people from ethnic minority backgrounds, and getting them into careers, rather than just jobs. Their specialist area, as denoted by the name, was housing, so they'd help people from ethnic minorities to work in local authority housing departments, and things like that.

Through them, I got an interview to work for an organisation working with the homeless called Thames Reach. Despite the fact that I turned up late, the panel really liked me, above many other candidates who had qualifications. They offered me a job there and then, as a trainee, even though I had no experience behind me. There was one small issue though – because I'd come to them through the PATH agency, no one seemed to have mentioned my criminal record. Somehow, I got away with it, and even managed to start work without anyone there finding out.

However, after working there for a month, I felt that, for integrity's sake, it was important that I came clean, even if it cost me this new and exciting job. I knew that integrity was something which God required of me, and so I took my boss to one side, and not only explained my offence, but also told her about what God had done in my life, and the change that had taken place. To her credit, and to my surprise, she decided that since I'd come clean with her, she'd take me at face value and keep me on. It hardly needs saying but, again, I saw this as God's providence.

For a year I worked there helping resettle people who had been sleeping rough on the streets of London. My role was very much hands on, working with people themselves, which really ticked my box in terms of doing real, gritty care work, and genuinely helping people. After that, I moved up in the organisation, becoming one of the core workers, and helping rough sleepers in some of the most notorious areas in London, including the Waterloo 'Bullring' and the area around the Savoy Hotel. As I worked there, it was a time when the organisation was gaining a very good reputation, and so, by association, my reputation was also being enhanced.

So from being a manslaughter convict just a few years earlier, now I had become a top figure in an important government agency. Only God can make things like that happen.

ELEVEN

It was 1997, and I was still part of the church in Walthamstow. The pastor who had helped Sheila and I through our most difficult times was looking to move on, and as one of the leaders, I was seen as one of the pillars of what was a small church. Some of the leadership team also decided that the time was right to move on, and so, despite still having a full-time job with the homeless agency, I became one of five people in the second tier of leadership in the church. I was the youngest and newest one, although many of the others had also recently joined. This was a big learning curve for me as it was for all of us. Many of us were people who had never had any experience of leadership. All our training was literally done on the job, in the church.

Within a year, the pastor had left. Rather than install another pastor, the regional overseer responsible for our network of churches came alongside us and asked if, between us, we'd be able to carry the church. And it wasn't really a question. He gave us some direction, and met with us once a month for about four months, just to make sure that we were on track. After that, though, we were left with total responsibility for the church until another pastor could come in.

At that time, God spoke to me clearly and told me that I was to change churches, and move to Emmanuel Christian Centre, which was also in Walthamstow. He didn't say when, but he was crystal clear that this was where I was meant to go. I told Sheila but nobody else, and we prayed about it. God spoke to me again, and confirmed the destination, but also told me that the time was not yet right. It had only been about a month since our pastor had left when God spoke, and another leader had stepped down, so there were only four of us left. The last thing the church needed at that time was another leader stepping down. So while I really felt God's vision was that I was definitely going to go to Emmanuel, it had to be the right time.

I was at the church for another year in the leadership role. At times it was quite hard for me because I was often in two minds: one thinking about the church I was in and the other about Emmanuel. When things were going well in church I could easily plough on and keep faithful and consistent. When things weren't going so well, a small church can contain a lot of problems and I would feel the

itch to move on. God really had to keep me focussed
and challenge me in that year. Eventually, the
denomination appointed a pastor to come in and
take over the church. I gave him four months to find
his feet, but then I approached him, inviting him
and his wife round to dinner. I took that opportunity to explain what I felt God had said to me, more
than a year previously, about moving to the other
church. I had made sure about it though. I had gone
to speak to someone who I held in high esteem: an
experienced Bible teacher who I really respected. He
said that he didn't advocate somebody moving from
church to church, but he could also see that this
wasn't a flash in the pan, but something I'd had on
my heart for over a year.

Also, I'd become involved with prison ministry,
so I paid a visit to Holy Trinity Brompton, the
church which birthed the Alpha course, to find out
about their 'Alpha for Prisons' course. The man who
was speaking announced that it was time for all of
us to pray, at which point a guy who I'd never met
before came up and asked if he could pray for me.
He did, and as he prayed he just started to say
things about my life that he couldn't possibly have
known. He was speaking prophetically – or rather,
God was speaking to me through him. He told me,
'God knows and sees that you have got to make a

decision. It is going to be hard, but he is with you, and he is going to stay with you.' As he prayed, I felt certain that this was God telling me that the time had arrived.

When I told the new pastor, he was shocked and saddened. 'No, no,' he said. 'Pray about it, think about it once more.'

Out of respect, I did as he had asked, but I had already made a decision based on what God had said to me. Two weeks later, I went back to him and explained that we were still going to move on. Although he didn't agree with it, he did then accept and respect our decision.

I put my actual departure date from the church in his hands, and he asked me to stay for another three months, which I happily agreed to do. When that period expired, in late 1999, we moved to Emmanuel Christian Centre. Having moved out of a small church and a position of leadership, it would be great just to relax, learn and receive for a while.

As I moved to Emmanuel, I began to feel something tugging at my heart, telling me that I was going to work in full-time Christian ministry. I'd felt that call faintly for a little while, but with three children, little experience, and no theological training, I wasn't quite sure how it would be possible.

I continued simply attending ECC for a few months and got to know some of the people. Over the years, I'd had some contact with a youth pastor called Dave. I'd gone along to a few of the events that he'd put on for young people, where I had been asked to tell a condensed version of my story. Out of the blue, he turned around and asked me if I'd be interested in coming on board and joining his youth work team. I went away and prayed about this, although I had a rumbling feeling in my being that it was right. I went back to him and expressed interest, and although I didn't over-commit myself, I did agree to become part of his team.

I started going along to the youth group sessions, which I enjoyed and felt very natural in. It was good to be part of the team as a volunteer, and I felt that I could really relate to some of the young people there. Many of them were going through similar struggles to those which I had faced ten years earlier, and I relished the opportunity to use my own experience to point them gently in the right direction. However, only six months into my role, Dave announced t hat he was thinking about going away to plant a church.

A few weeks after that, he came to see me.

'Dez,' he said warmly, 'I think that you're the man to take over my job.'

'Whoa!' I was caught off guard. 'I'm not sure about that!' I'd only just started doing voluntary youth work – surely it was too early to be thinking about full-time work?

'Alright, Dez,' said Dave, understanding my reaction. 'Let's both go away and pray about this.'

And so we did. What followed was not an instantaneous decision but a period of many weeks where we discussed, prayed and thought. Over that time, I got a chance to shadow him in his work, and slowly it all began to make sense; I was in the frame, and it clicked.

God said to me, 'Wherever you go, Dez, you are going to be blessed.' I read, because he showed me, a part of the Bible where Abraham and Lot go their separate ways after their plans become too big side by side. Because God has blessed him, Abraham has become so confident that he can ask Lot which way he wants to go, and be comfortable with the other way. Lot obviously looks at the land that seems to be plentiful and vibrant and full of growth and decides he's going there. Even though Abraham basically gets second choice, he isn't concerned because he knows that whether he goes east or west he is going to be blessed, because he has got God's hands on him. That's what God told me. His hands were on me, and whatever I chose to do was going to prosper because he had blessed me. In the past, I'd always felt that God was guiding me in certain directions, but here it was different. God seemed to be saying to me – 'It's your shout Dez.'

I made my choice. I spoke to the pastor, and met with the elders of the church. They gave me the thumbs up. In 2001, I took the job on a part-time basis. I was working with the homeless at the same time, although obviously I scaled down my hours with them. Fortunately, they didn't want to lose me and were willing to accommodate me wherever possible. They knew that I was a core team member because in that line of work the average work span is about two years, due to the stress and pressures of working with that type of client. I had been there for nearly five years, and because of all my knowledge and all the things that I'd been through and seen, they didn't want me to leave altogether.

That was great for a year, but eventually the conflicts of juggling two people-focussed jobs and a family became a strain. I decided that I would leave my work with the homeless behind, and move into youth work full-time – a role which the church duly offered me, and which I'm still doing today.

My journey, which had seen me start out as a young offender, had now taken me to a strange and miraculous place. Now I – who once had looked like I was heading into a life of crime – was entrusted with a full-time position, acting as a guide and role model for young people. If that isn't a testimony to the power of God, I'm not sure what is!

It wasn't quite true that I was now working with young people who were just like I used to be, though. The majority of the twenty to twenty-five teenagers in the church youth group that Dave had left behind were church children, and few of them had been through anything like the experiences I'd gone through as a teenager. Still, although they weren't 'bad' kids, they were hardly 'on fire' with passion for God either. I realised that many of these young people had been brought up in church, but most of them didn't actually pray. Or, at least, they didn't know how to pray. Straight away I made the decision that we'd hold a prayer meeting every week for the young people, because prayer is fundamental to young people's growth as Christians. It has happened every Wednesday since and, although we don't attract massive numbers, a core of around six to ten young people faithfully turn up to pray each week. This meeting has become key to all we do as a youth group, as a steadily increasing number of young people decide to get to a deeper level with God.

Alongside my work with young people, I also work in prisons, where I speak at specially-arranged gatherings and chapel meetings, sharing the story of how God changed my life. Because I've been there, where they're sitting, and because I speak their language, they quieten down and listen – especially when they hear that I wasn't just in there for fraud or unpaid fines, but for manslaughter. I continue to have many great opportunities to share my story across the country, both in prisons and at youth meetings.

On top of all that, and perhaps most surprisingly of all, I've become a reverend in the Assemblies of God (AOG) denomination. That wasn't just some kind of Internet ordination – I had to write a series of essays and reports over two years, and be assessed on my preaching ability. At the moment, though, that's not truly something that causes my heart to beat, and I have never really seen myself as a pastor. I simply tell the story to illustrate just how far God has brought me.

In a little over a decade, I have gone from being a selfish, inwardly-focussed, proud, sinful teenager who ended another man's life, to a youth pastor and a reverend. From a young offender, God formed a youth leader. From a prisoner, he formed a prisons evangelist. From a rotten, sinful, manipulative scoundrel, he brought life and restoration and love. I was convicted but I was not condemned, and now the miracles God has done in my life point back to him and demonstrate how real and involved and incredible he is.

TWELVE

That's my story – or at least, my story so far. As you've read it, you may have felt empathy, cynicism, something in between or nothing at all. When we read about someone's experience with God, we can look at that life and think – *'Well, that's just an extreme experience. My personal experience is nothing like that.'* Perhaps you've read my story and think that I needed God because of all the bad things I have done.

Although I have done a lot of bad things, God sees all the wrong that I've done on the same par as everybody else's wrong. As hard as this might be to swallow, to God there isn't really a difference between someone who has committed a murder and someone who's done an aggravated burglary, or someone who has manipulated somebody else. He doesn't put levels on it – and unless it's dealt with, the sentence for every wrong is exactly the same, and there's no parole. To God, sin is sin; wrong is wrong. There are different consequences to the different kinds of wrong which we do, but wrong has to be accounted for.

If you look at your own life, do you realise that somewhere along the line you have done wrong? Have you ever consciously gone out of your way and knowingly done wrong? If that's you, and I'm pretty sure it describes every single person bar one who ever walked this earth, the message that I want to give to you is this: Jesus Christ paid the price for that wrong. In a sense, when he was nailed to that cross, the nails went into his hands for my manslaughter, but also for my manipulation. When those nails went into his hands they did so for my deceit, for my theft, for my lies. Nobody but me would have seen all of that – all the court would have looked at is the manslaughter – but God saw everything. How much of your life does God see?

You may think, '*That's good for you Dez, you changed,*' but I want to tell you that I couldn't have done it on my own. I want to say to you that wherever you are, you too need to make that decision to change. God even knows your heart at this moment, and he is right beside you, so close that you could almost reach out and touch him. He's waiting for you to ask him to change you, too.

I never chose God. There is a verse in the Bible that says we never chose God but God chose us. You didn't pick this book up by chance. So if you have read the story and your heart is beating; if you're thinking that you believe what I'm saying but you're not sure you could change, then don't be afraid. There's no way that I could have changed either, but God changed me, and the first step in all of that was that I let him into my life. You can do that now.

There is a famous statement used by people who have either been alcoholics or drug addicts. They say, 'Take each day as it comes'. I think it's the same with Christianity, especially in the early stages. You have got to take each day as it comes, and that means committing every day to God; every day saying, 'God I need more of your grace, I need more of your help.' We all get good days and we all get bad days, but the important thing, just as my story shows, is to keep on going – to keep on rising each time we fall.

We need to break away from the nature and the mindset that society has grown in us like a cancer, but we can't do that through our own will. We can only do it through the power of the Holy Spirit, God's helper here on earth. If you accept Jesus into your life today, you are going to be filled with a measure of the Holy Spirit who is going to work in you. That's what can change you – God himself working from within you. Initially, what God wants to do is change your heart. He wants to change the way you see life, the way you see yourself, and the way you see him, so that you can gain a true and accurate perspective on all those things.

Whether we want to or not we are all going to die, and we are all going to meet God. Whether you do that as his friend, or as a stranger, is up to you. Where will you spend eternity? There are two options – either you spend it with God or you spend it eternally separated from him. That question can be decided today. You don't have to wait until you meet him, because when you do it might just be too late.

* * *

If, after reading all that, you would like to do something about it right now and ask Jesus into your life, then right where you are, just pray these words along with me:

Jesus, I recognise that I have done wrong. I recognise that I have lived wrongly. But today I realise that there is a right way to live. Please forgive me of all the wrong that I have done and to come into my life. What I mean, Lord, is that I want you to help me to make my decisions. I want to involve you in my future, and in my present, but I ask you to wipe away my past – all the bad things that

I have done – and no longer hold it against me. And so, please come into my life right now, and change me from within.

In Jesus' name,
Amen.

More Than a Carpenter

His story might change yours

Josh McDowell &
Sean McDowell

Josh McDowell's examination of the true nature of Christ and
his impact on our lives is a modern classic, having sold over
15 million copies. Now updated and revised with his son Sean
McDowell, it has new content that addresses questions raised by
today's popular atheist writers.

Written by a skeptic turned believer, *More Than a Carpenter*
challenges readers to ask the question, 'Who is Jesus?' Author and
renowned speaker Josh McDowell acknowledges that while the
topic of God is widely accepted, the name of Jesus often causes
irritation. 'Why don't the names of Buddha, Mohammed,
Confucius offend people? The reason is that these others didn't
claim to be God, but Jesus did.'

By addressing questions about scientific and historical evidence,
the validity of the Bible, and proofs of the resurrection, the
authors help the reader come to an informed and intelligent
decision about whether Jesus was a liar, a lunatic, or the Lord.

978-1-85078-846-1

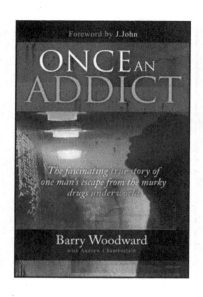

Once an Addict

The fascinating true story of one man's escape from the murky drugs underworld

Barry Woodward
with Andrew Chamberlain

Barry Woodward was a drug dealer and heroin addict who once lived on the notorious Bull Rings in the centre of Manchester. *Once an Addict* describes Barry's descent into the murky underworld of drug dealing, addiction, crime and imprisonment. Along the way we are intro-duced to some of the most extraordinary characters, and we see the extreme lengths to which some of them will go to get their next 'fix'. Illegal drug use claimed the lives of many such people, and it seemed inevitable that Barry would also succumb to the consequences of his addic-tion.

With devastating amphetamine-induced mental health issues, a fourteen-year heroin addiction, a string of bro-ken relationships, and the threat of HIV looming, the outlook for Barry appeared very bleak. Then three extraordinary encounters changed his life forever . . .

978-1-86024-602-9

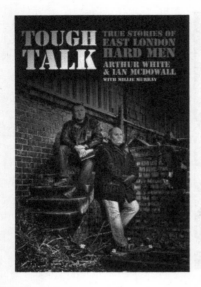

Tough Talk

True stories of east London hard men

*Arthur White and Ian McDowall
with Millie Murray*

Arthur's Story

World champion powerlifter, successful businessman, happy family man. But Arthur's life spiralled out of con-trol. Cocaine, steroids and an affair ruined everything and he lost his business, family – all the things that were really important. Death seemed the only way out. What changed him?

Ian's Story

Body building was Ian's life and he was determined to become No.1 at all costs. Being a doorman and debt col-lector enabled him to sustain his use of illegal steroids. Cheating in his sport, robbing on the door – Ian's days were filled with violence and deceit. What changed him?

978-1-86024-823-8

Tough Talk 2

More life-changing stories from the Tough Talk team

with
Millie Murray

Joe Lampshire – '"YOU WILL DIE" . . . Playing the Ouija board was just for a laugh; I had done it many times before. But this was something way, way out of my experience and it wasn't funny.' For Joe, this was just the beginning of a long battle with the spirit world. As dark forces threatened to claim Joe's life, could light ever break through?

Martyn Parrish – 'It was heady stuff and, of course, I wan-ted to do it again. I wanted to drop some pills and then ride my bike. This was living! Or so I thought.' At first the drugs freed Martyn's mind, and then they began to completely take over. As heroin became Martyn's closest and most destructive friend, could he ever find peace?

Simon Pinchbeck – 'I'd been greedy, thinking how much I'd make out of my investment, and now it was gone. I felt the need to settle the matter, preferably by slowly killing each man involved.' A hunger for money and involvement with tough and violent police corps had sent Simon's life spiralling out of control. Deserted by friends and in huge debt, would he ever find a way out?

978-1-86024-700-2

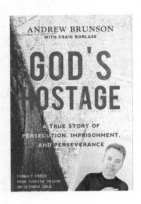

God's Hostage

*A True Story of Persecution,
Imprisonment and Perseverance*

Andrew Brunson

735 days in a Turkish prison for a crime he did not commit.

When God called, Andrew Brunson answered and went to Turkey as a missionary. Accused of being a spy and a plotter of an attempted coup, Andrew became a political pawn whose story soon became known around the world.

This is the incredible true story of Andrew's imprisonment, his brokenness, his faithfulness … and his freedom.

978-1-78893-127-4

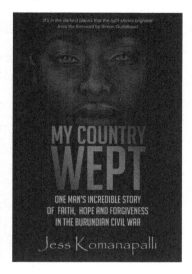

My Country Wept

One man's incredible story of faith, hope and forgiveness in the Burundian civil war

Jess Komanapalli

Theodore Mbazumutima was forced to flee from his native Burundi when tensions between Hutus and Tutsis escalated. Theo's dangerous and incredible journey fleeing the civil war is an amazing testimony of God's miraculous interven-tion, protection and guidance.

Despite experiencing suffering first hand, God has brought Theo to such a place of forgiveness that he is now a peace worker bringing reconciliation to the Burundian people.

My Country Wept reminds us that when we submit to God's plans for our lives, he can rescue us from any circumstance and work in every situation.

978-1-78078-464-9

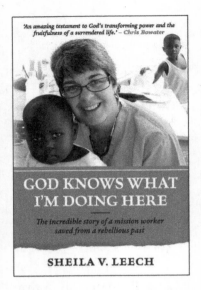

God Knows What I'm Doing Here

The incredible story of a mission worker saved from a rebellious past

Sheila Leech

Sheila Leech's Sunday school teacher would plead with God, 'Please don't let Sheila come to class today!' As a teenager, she was far from God and taking drugs – until Jesus broke into her life and called her into his service.

For nine years she lived with an indigenous tribe in the Ecuadorian rainforest as a missionary. Having trained as a nurse, she now travels the world serving those affected by war and natural disasters.

A gripping account of her sometimes perilous adventures, Sheila's story demonstrates God's grace and protection, his power and provision, and that he can use anyone who trusts in him, whatever their start in life.

978-1-78078-452-6

Blood, Sweat and Jesus

*The story of a Christian hospital
bringing hope and healing in a
Muslim community*

Kerry Stillman

What is a Christian hospital doing in a remote Muslim area of
Cameroon?

Kerry Stillman shares her own experiences of working as a
physiotherapist in a sub-Saharan village hospital. A vivid
impression of daily life is painted as the team deal with the threat
of terrorism, the attitudes of local people towards Western
medicine, their patients' health issues, and the challenge of
sensitively sharing the gospel in a different culture.

Passionate, intriguing and uplifting, this is a colourful
interweaving of cultures, beliefs and the power of prayer
alongside modern medicine.

978-1-78893-148-9

Ever Present

*Running to survive, thrive
and believe*

Austen Hardwick

Strokes, brain surgery, epilepsy . . . where is God in the middle of our suffering?

After surviving three strokes in his forties, Austen Hardwick began to think more deeply about life and faith. As he started to recover, he realised that running created space in which he could draw closer to God.

Weaving together personal testimony and biblical teaching, Austen encourages us to run towards God rather than away from him, so that we, too, can learn to live life in all its fullness with an ever-present God who is with us in our struggles.

Genuine, real, and inspirational, Ever Present explores how running can be good for both the heart and the soul.

978-1-78893-136-6

Authentic

We trust you enjoyed reading this book from Authentic. If you want to be informed of any new titles from this author and other releases you can sign up to the Authentic newsletter by scanning below:

Online:
authenticmedia.co.uk

Follow us: